The Third Age Trust

The Third Age Trust is the body which represents all U3As in the UK. The U3A movement is made up of over 700 self-governing groups of older men and women who organise for themselves activities which may be educational, recreational or social in kind. Calling on their own experience and knowledge they demand no qualifications nor do they offer any. The movement has grown at a remarkable pace and offers opportunities to thousands of people to demonstrate their own worth to one another and to the community. Their interests are astonishingly varied but the members all value the opportunity to share experiences and learning with like-minded people. The Third Age Trust's endorsement of the Older and Wiser series hints at some of that width of interest.

THE THIRD AGE TRUST

U3A

THE UNIVERSITY OF THE THIRD AGE

Social Networking for the Older and Wiser

Connect with Family and Friends, Old and New

Sean McManus

A John Wiley and Sons, Ltd., Publication

This edition first published 2010
© 2010 Sean McManus

Registered office
John Wiley & Sons Ltd, The Atrium, Southern Gate, Chichester, West Sussex, PO19 8SQ, United Kingdom

For details of our global editorial offices, for customer services and for information about how to apply for permission to reuse the copyright material in this book please see our website at www.wiley.com.

Microsoft product screenshots reprinted with permission from Microsoft Corporation.

Wiley also publishes its books in a variety of electronic formats. Some content that appears in print may not be available in electronic books.

All website information (such as privacy settings and terms & conditions) correct at time of going to press. Please check appropriate website for current details.

A catalogue record for this book is available from the British Library.

ISBN 978-0-470-68640-9

Set in 11/13 Zapf Humanist 601 BT by Laserwords Private Limited, Chennai, India
Printed in Great Britain by Bell & Bain, Glasgow

Dedication

To my older and wisers: Mum and Dad, and Brian and Wylda

Contents

Chapter 5 – Using Twitter to tell the world what you're doing

Contents

Acknowledgements

Thank you to my wonderful wife Karen for her support throughout this project. The team on this book includes (in order of appearance) Chris Webb (acquisitions editor), Neil Salkind (agent), Ellie Scott (publishing assistant), Sydney Jones (development editor), Rachel Clarke (technical editor), Juliet Booker (project editor), Steve Long (cartoonist), Sarah Lewis (copy editor), Claire Spinks (content editor), and Sarah Price (proofreader). For help with research, thank you to Doreen Howell, Pam Fitchett, Jane Green, Fiona Campbell-Howes, and everyone who responded to our permissions requests and research queries. Special thanks to the Internet pioneers who created the social networks I use to keep in touch with my friends and family.

About the Author

Sean McManus is a technology and business author. His previous books include 'Small Business Websites That Work' and a novel about the music industry called 'University of Death'. His tutorials and articles have appeared in magazines including *Internet Magazine*, *Internet Works*, *Business 2.0*, *Making Music*, *Melody Maker* and *Personal Computer World*. He created Wild Mood Swings (**www.wildmoodswings.co.uk**), a web toy that shows you websites to match your mood, and blogs regularly on his personal website at **www.sean.co.uk**.

Publisher's Acknowledgements

Some of the people who helped bring this book to market include the following:

Editorial and Production
VP Consumer and Technology Publishing Director: Michelle Leete
Associate Director – Book Content Management: Martin Tribe
Associate Publisher: Chris Webb
Assistant Editor: Colleen Goldring
Publishing Assistant: Ellie Scott
Content Editor: Claire Spinks
Project Editor: Juliet Booker
Development Editor: Sydney Jones
Technical Editor: Rachel Clarke
Copy Editor: Sarah Lewis

Marketing
Senior Marketing Manager: Louise Breinholt
Marketing Executive: Chloe Tunnicliffe

Composition Services
Compositor: Laserwords Private Limited
Proofreader: Sarah Price
Indexer: Geraldine Begley

With thanks to U3A member, Mrs Gillian Brown, for naming our Older and Wiser owl 'Steady Stanley'. This was the winning entry from the U3A News competition held in October 2009.

Icons used in this book

Throughout this book, we've used icons to help focus your attention on certain information. This is what they mean:

Equipment needed	Lets you know in advance the equipment you will need to hand as you progress through the chapter.
Skills needed	Placed at the beginning to help identify the skills you'll need for the chapter ahead.
Tip	Tips and suggestions to help make life easier.
Note	Take note of these little extras to avoid confusion.
Warning	Read carefully; a few things could go wrong at this point.
Try It	Go on, enjoy yourself; you won't break it.
Trivia	A little bit of fun to bring a smile to your face.
Summary	A short recap at the end of each chapter.
Brain Training	Test what you've learned from the chapter.

PRACTICE MAKES
PERFECT

To build upon the lessons learnt in this book, visit www.pcwisdom.co.uk

- More training tutorials

- Links to resources

- Advice through frequently asked questions

- Social networking tips

- Videos and podcasts from the author

- Author blogs

PART I
Getting started

It's amazing how many other people out there are into Star Trek, growing dahlias and listening to bagpipe music!

Introducing social networking

Equipment needed: Access to a computer (desktop or laptop) with an Internet connection; your own email address.

Skills needed: Some basic experience of using a computer, enthusiasm and an open mind.

For years now, the Internet has been bringing people together: best friends who lost touch after graduation, families divided by oceans, and former colleagues who went their separate ways. Online, they can rediscover each other, chat, play games, and share photos and videos. School reunions can be orchestrated, from tracking down the old sixth form through to sending out invitations and sharing the post-event photos. Current friends can keep in touch more easily, and plan their get-togethers, and strangers with common interests can seek and share advice, and celebrate their successes.

So what allows people to come together in this way? Social networking sites make all this possible. You might have heard talk of Facebook, Friends Reunited or Twitter and wondered what the fuss was about, or didn't even understand what on earth they were. Perhaps younger family members are already using these sites, and want to keep in touch with you using them, but you simply don't know how.

Using this book, you'll learn how to use the Internet to make new friends and how you can reconnect with old friends you've lost touch with. Whether you've already made a start with sites like Facebook, or you're new to the whole concept of social networking, this book will introduce you to some of the leading places you can connect with friends online. By the end of the book, you will have the confidence and skills to explore other social networking sites out there. Social networking sites are powerful tools, but they are easy to use. Some familiarity with using a computer, access to an Internet-enabled computer and an email address are all you need to get started.

The book is divided into three parts. Part I introduces you to the basic idea of social networking, and the general procedures and techniques needed to begin. You will learn how to log in to a network, create an account, and complete an online profile. The techniques learnt here will be required for all the sites considered in this book, so take your time to get the basics right.

Part II introduces you to some of the best-known and most widely used social networks: Facebook (in Chapter 3), Friends Reunited (in Chapter 4), and Twitter (in Chapter 5). You will see how to use the skills you have acquired in Part I of the book to find old friends, make new ones, and post messages.

In Part III, you'll learn how to connect with other older and wisers at Saga Zone (Chapter 6) and Eons (Chapter 7). You will discover how to use Meetup (Chapter 8) to organise get-togethers in the real world, and the most advanced topic of all – how to create your very own, personalised network using Ning (Chapter 9). If you participate in a local group (such as a U3A group, Probus, or a writers' circle), you can use Ning and Meetup to create a private social network for your members. Alternatively, you could also use them to start a new network dedicated to your hobby, and recruit members online and from your address book.

If you're new to the Internet, there is an appendix at the back of the book that will take you from your first click through to being an internet wizard. You can refer to this at any time, or give it a quick read now if you'd like to brush up your web skills before diving into social networking. It will also show you how you can magnify webpages and use keyboard shortcuts, for if you struggle with the text on screen and with the mouse.

I'll try to keep the jargon to a minimum, but as with everything to do with computers, some of it will be unavoidable. The book contains a glossary at the back to provide a quick reminder if you forget what a key term means, or if you come across a phrase you're not familiar with.

You may be surprised to know that there are many more social networking sites out there, just waiting to be discovered. So at the end of the book, you can find a directory of new places to explore.

As this book is intended as an introduction to social networking, it's not possible to cover every feature of social networking. You may be interested in checking out some additional resources in support of this book by going to my own website, **www.sean.co.uk**. There you will find bonus content there wasn't room for here, and all the links used so you can save time typing them in. Take your time. The book covers a wide scope and you will need practice at each stage to gain in both competence and confidence. Read on to make a start . . .

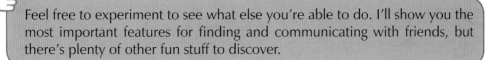

Feel free to experiment to see what else you're able to do. I'll show you the most important features for finding and communicating with friends, but there's plenty of other fun stuff to discover.

What is social networking?

The term 'social network' has been coined for websites that give you tools to help you communicate with your social circle and find new friends. You may not realise that family members and friends are possibly already online at these websites, waiting for you to connect with them.

Here are some of the things you can do using social networking sites:

● Find old friends you lost touch with, from school or work.

● Bring together groups of your current friends on the Internet so you can easily keep in touch with everyone.

● Make new friends, by introducing yourself to your friends' friends, or by finding others with similar interests and/or in your age group.

● Share albums of photos and videos, and let your friends and relatives add their comments to them.

● Have discussions with friends and strangers about life, the universe and everything.

- Play games against your friends over the Internet.

- Broadcast what you're doing or reading to the world, by sending out status updates in real time.

- Keep in touch with what your favourite celebrities are doing, and send them messages.

- Find events that you can attend to socialise in the real world, or use social networking tools to organise and promote your own events.

If you're new to all this, it might seem odd to socialise with people who aren't even in the same room as you, maybe not even in the same country. But if you use email already, you can think of social networking as an extension of that. Instead of having communications going from one person to another, your conversations can take place in a more public space, where your mutual friends can chip in. It's a bit like being in a room full of friends, with everyone jumping in with their thoughts, jokes and memories.

Communicating this way might sound a bit daunting but don't worry because although some of the activities on social networking sites take place in public, or at least in front of your friends, you can still have private conversations and share private information with people. As we explore social networking websites together, you'll learn the privacy implications of the different activities: who can see what, who can find you, and who can find out what you're doing.

So why bother to use social networking sites? People like social networking for different reasons. If you're geographically isolated, or if you're unable to travel far, social networking can enable you to build close friendships without even leaving the house. Some people like the fact that they can switch on the computer at any time and see what their friends have been up to. For others, it's about being able to share their creative work, and their ideas, with a global audience. You might most enjoy being able to talk about your hobbies and interests with people who share your passion. That certainly stops me having to bore my real-world friends with my own particular enthusiasm for Prince 12" remixes and vintage arcade games!

As we take a tour through some of the most popular social networking sites, you will discover your own ways to make social networking enhance your life, online and offline. Perhaps you'll rediscover a friend from decades ago. Maybe you'll find a new hobby, or start a romantic relationship? Anything is possible!

What you need

Throughout this book, I am assuming that you have already acquired the basic skills of using a computer, keyboard and mouse. To get started with social networking, you need access to a computer, an Internet connection, an email address, and some familiarity with the Internet.

A computer

The beauty of social networking is that you can do it using virtually any computer type with an Internet connection. For the examples presented in this book, I've used a PC (personal computer) running Windows Vista. If you're using a Mac or a different version of Windows, you'll find your screens sometimes look a little different, but don't worry as you should still be able to benefit from all the guidance in this book.

You don't necessarily need your own computer: you might be able to use one in the library, although you'll find it easier to keep in regular contact with your online friends if you have your own PC. Photo uploading can be much more time-consuming on public computers, too, because you probably won't have permission to install the software needed for bulk uploading (more on this later, in Chapter 3).

An Internet connection

To gain access to social networking sites, your computer needs to be connected to the Internet. As well as having a cable between the computer and the wall socket, you'll need to subscribe to an Internet Service Provider (ISP), which does the same job as a phone company like BT does for telephones: it connects you to the communications network. In fact, most phone companies provide Internet services too, so if you don't already have an ISP, contact your phone company and they can probably help you get connected. The cost of being connected to the Internet can vary depending on the company you use, so you may be able to save money by shopping around before making a decision.

You have two main types of Internet connection to choose from:

● *Dial-up* connections require you to 'phone up' the ISP each time you want to use the Internet or email. For light users of the Internet, dial-up connections can be cheaper, but they come with the disadvantage of being rather slow.

- *Broadband* connections are always switched on. That means you can just go into a website whenever you want, straight away. There's no need to wait for the computer to connect to the ISP. Broadband can be over 20 times faster than dial-up. If you want to use video or music websites, broadband is essential. The snag is that it isn't available everywhere, depending on where you live, and it does cost a little more, but again, you should check out the availability and rates of different companies to help you decide.

For most social networking, it doesn't really matter whether you've got dial-up or broadband. You'll have more fun on broadband, though. There will be less hanging around, and you can be more spontaneous. If you've got the choice between a Ferrari and an old banger that you have to start up by cranking the handle, why not opt for the smoother ride?

If you are able to use your computer to download email or to visit websites like the BBC site (**www.bbc.co.uk**), then you've definitely got a working Internet connection already.

Make sure your computer is protected with a *firewall* (to stop other people snooping on your PC when you're connected to the Internet) and *antivirus software* (to eradicate malicious programs that try to get access to your data or corrupt your PC). Security suites include antivirus software and a firewall, and can be bought in high-street computer retailers as well as through online stores like Amazon. You don't necessarily need to splash out, though. You can get free antivirus software from AVG (**free.avg.com**), and Windows XP, Windows Vista and Windows 7 all have a built-in firewall. Security software is essential whenever you're connected to the Internet, and the threat is equally high whether or not you're using social networking sites.

An email address

Your email address is used in social networking to forward messages from your friends on to you, and to alert you to updates within your network. For that reason, you'll need to have a working email address to sign up to most social networks. They won't let you in if you don't have one, or if you refuse to tell them what it is.

You're unlikely to have a problem with receiving lots of junk emails. The big social networks explored in this book are well-established businesses, and they won't abuse your email address for a quick buck. Their reputation is worth too much to them for that to be a smart move.

You should consider setting up a new email account to protect your privacy. Your email address can reveal all kinds of things about you, including where you work (if you use a work email address) and even where you live (if you have your own website). If you're not comfortable with that information being available to some of your friends online, you can register a more anonymous email account for free through **www.googlemail.com**. Having all your social network correspondence in one place might make it easier to manage, too.

Some familiarity with the Internet

You don't need fancy technical skills to take advantage of social networking, but you do need some familiarity with the Internet. If you've used a website before for shopping, email, researching holidays, or similar activities, you have all the skills you need.

If you haven't used the Internet before don't worry, it really doesn't take too long to learn. See Appendix A for a tutorial, which will take you from your first click to mastering your browser. See also *The Internet for the Older and Wiser* by Adrian Arnold, another book in this series, for a comprehensive guide to using the Internet.

Overcoming common fears

When embarking on something new, it's natural to have some reservations. Sometimes scare stories in the newspapers about the Internet can alarm us, but if our world view were defined by the tabloids, we'd be terrified to climb out from under the duvet. I'd like to start by reassuring you about some of the most common fears people have about social networking.

When you arrive at the social network, you should see an invitation to join or sign up. They're pretty keen to recruit new members, so the link or button is usually large, but it is sometimes hidden in some small text at the top of the screen.

The network walks you through creating your account by asking you to enter information into a series of short forms. The information requested varies by network, but typically includes the following:

- **Email address:** Messages from the network and from your friends will be sent to you at this address. This is so important, you're often asked to type it twice to make sure there's no mistake.

- **Password:** To protect your personal information, choose a memorable password that nobody else can work out. Avoid dictionary words, names, and things that could easily be guessed from your profile (such as Ringo, if you say you're a Beatles fan). One way to come up with an obscure password is to think of the first line of a favourite song and use the initial letters from the words in it. From the nursery rhyme 'Jack and Jill went up the hill', you can make the password 'jajwuth', for example. The longer the password, the stronger it is. Using numbers and punctuation increases the security, too.

- **Username:** Some sites use pseudonyms in place of your real name on the site. This can help to protect your privacy. Usernames must usually be unique, so if someone else already has your preferred username, you must come up with a variation on it.

- **Date of birth:** This can be used to check you're old enough to join, ensure the adverts on the site are relevant, and remind your friends to send you a birthday card. Some people prefer to give false information to protect their identity because a date of birth makes it easier for companies to combine marketing data from different sources. If you fib, make sure you remember what you said. Your birth date is often used to recover your account if you lose your password or email address.

Passing the security checks

Before sites will let you register, they usually ask you to pass a security check. The so-called *captcha*, as shown in Figure 2.1, aims to catch out those people (known as 'spammers') who use programs to invent fake accounts. The idea is that if you can pass this simple test, you're a human and not a program, so you're allowed in.

Security Check

Enter **both words** below, **separated by a space.**

Can't read the words below? Try different words or an audio captcha.

silkens compaigns

Text in the box:

◄ **Back** | **Sign Up** |

By clicking Sign Up, you are indicating that you have read and agree to the Terms of Use and Privacy Policy.

Reproduced by permission of Facebook

Figure 2.1

To pass the test, you just have to read the slightly distorted words and type them into the box. Don't worry – it's not your eyes. Sometimes the words become too mangled to be read, so if that's happened to you, just use the link provided to request some new words. If it's any consolation, it often takes me two (or more) goes to get it right.

The Recaptcha-branded puzzles (used at Eons – see Chapter 7) also get you to do a bit of manual labour at the same time. One of the words is there to test you're a real person before allowing you to create an account, as usual, but the other one is taken from a book that's been scanned and needs to be converted into text. All the 5-second chunks of time people spend solving captchas can then be used to digitise old books, to help the spread of knowledge.

At some point in the registration process, you'll also be asked to click a link that is emailed to you. This proves that you do own the email account you're trying to register with.

Creating your profile

Your profile is an overview of who you are, and you create it by entering information about yourself into various forms. The basics are usually gathered during registration, but after registration it's a good idea to go into your profile and edit it to add more detail. It reassures friends looking for you that they've found the right person, and makes it easier to find people with similar interests.

Profiles vary greatly from site to site. Facebook provides you with space to detail your past schools and employers, as well as your favourite films, books, music, and interests (as covered in Chapter 3). You can enter information until your fingers are worn to stumps. At Twitter (see Chapter 5), you'll have to say who you are in just 160 characters. Choosing the right words against such a tight limit might take just as long!

Before entering anything sensitive, make sure you understand who will be able to read it. After all, the point of entering the information is to share it. Sometimes it's only available to those you have explicitly authorised to be your friends within the network, but other times it's available to anyone. As you explore each network in this book, I'll clarify who can see your information. You don't have to fill out everything, anyway. You can usually leave a box blank if you don't want to comment on it at all.

Adding your profile image

Many networks invite you to upload a digital photograph of yourself. Don't be put off by this, though, as it's meant to show your friends that they've found the right person, so it's an important tool for getting back in touch. Here are some tips for creating your perfect profile image:

- Make sure your picture is uncluttered. Don't use group photos. Ideally, it should be a photo that just shows you, against a reasonably clear background.

- Your profile photo will often appear quite small on the website, such as in search results. You need to be certain that your photo is still recognisably you, even when it's shrunk. For best results, use a shot of your face or head, rather than your full body. Certainly don't use a holiday photo of rolling hills, with you in the middle distance. You'll be a tiny blob.

- Don't use abstract images (such as a picture of your car). Your old friends are more likely to ignore you than send you a message to find out if you're the person they're looking for.

- Try not to change your image too often. People get accustomed to what your image looks like and this makes it easier for them to understand who's talking when you post things online – they can recognise your picture immediately.

- Once you've found a picture you're happy with, you can use the same one across all your social networking sites to save time. It will also make it easier for friends to recognise you if they befriend you on multiple social networks.

- If your photo is a large file (taken with a digital camera, for example), you can make it smaller at **www.shrinkpictures.com**. Twitter requires relatively small images (700K), and you can create these here. If you plan to use the same image across different sites, shrinking it can also save you time uploading to each one. If your photo is a good head and shoulders shot, a maximum size of 350 pixels should be ample.

- Oh, and don't forget to say "cheese"!

Be patient when your photos are uploading. If you are using a shot from your digital camera, it could be a large file that takes a minute or more to upload, particularly if you're using a dial-up connection.

Using your email address book to find your friends

When you first join a social network, one of the things you will want to do is find your friends there. You probably have your friends already organised and listed in the address book you use for email. Wouldn't it be good if social networks could just use that, to save you having to search for people? The good news is that many of them can.

If you use a website to manage your email, rather than using a program on your computer, social networks can often log into your email account and hoover up all your contact information. You can import contacts from email addresses provided by Yahoo, Hotmail, Googlemail (or Gmail), MSN, AOL, BT Internet, and many continental European and hobby-focused email providers, depending on which services the social network supports. You can add contacts from an email account even if it's not the one you have used to register with the social network.

You can add email contacts at:

- Facebook (hover over Friends on the navigation bar, or 'navbar', then select Find Friends from the pop-up menu).
- Twitter (click Find people on the main navbar, and then Find on other networks).
- Meetup (via Promote on the navbar).
- Ning (click Invite on the navbar).

To do this, you need to provide your email address and email password to the network, so it can log in on your behalf and gather your email contacts. I wouldn't normally recommend entering your password into any website except the website it's intended for, in this case your webmail provider. If you gave your webmail password to someone untrustworthy, it could be used to send unwanted emails ('spam') in your name.

The leading websites in this book have been handpicked and can be considered trustworthy. If other websites or programs ask you to provide security credentials for somewhere else, I recommend you err on the side of caution and withhold them.

Logging out to protect your account

When you've finished using a social network, you need to log out – especially if you're using a shared computer, such as in your local library. This stops others from having access to your account. You'll find the link to log out – or sign out – on nearly every page, often at the top right of the screen, and sometimes on the main navigation bar ('navbar') used to move through the website.

I recommend that you try to complete the process you're in the middle of before logging out (such as setting up a group, or publishing a photo), to avoid too much difficulty and repetition when you continue later.

When you next visit the social network site, you will need to enter your username or email address and your password to get back in. If you're logged onto a site on your computer at home and you subsequently leave the computer unattended, make sure there are no mischief-makers in your family first. I was surprised to see somebody I follow on Twitter add a post saying "I smell of turds and Chloe rocks". A few hours later, he deleted the post, adding that his daughter Chloe was now grounded.

If you can see somebody else's data when you visit a social network, it means the machine has been left logged on by someone else. Click to log out and you can then log into your own account.

Learning the culture of social networking

Social networks are a bit like a foreign country; they have a few customs and conventions that might prove confusing if you're not aware of them before you start.

In this section, I'll introduce you to some of the more commonly seen customs. Don't worry about remembering all this – it's here to refer to, and there will be people in your network who will be happy to help if you don't understand something.

Understanding netiquette

Many sites have their own set of guidelines, designed to ensure that the forums remain safe and friendly places for everyone who participates. Some of the same rules apply across most social networking sites. This set of guidelines is known as 'netiquette', a cut and shut of the words 'net' and 'etiquette'. It defines what 'good manners' means when people communicate on the Internet.

Most of the rules are common sense, but it's worth taking a brisk run-through before we start social networking properly, all the same:

● Do criticise opinions, but do not attack the people expressing them. Don't say: "You're a moron." Do say: "Your point of view overlooks this important fact . . ." The term 'flame' is used to refer to a vicious posting.

- Don't write anything untrue that might lower somebody's impression of a living person or group of people (libel). You could get yourself and the website in trouble.

- Don't post anything racist, pornographic, violent or otherwise likely to cause offence (including swearing). Remember, forums are public gatherings, so don't share anything you wouldn't be happy to say at a company outing or family barbecue.

- Don't start a fight. It's called 'trolling' when people post things purely to wind up other people on the forum, and it's frowned-upon. For example, going into a Beatles forum and saying "the Beatles never did anything any good".

- Don't post the same thing repeatedly in a forum, even in different categories or discussions. Find the best place for your post and put it there. If it doesn't get a response, it's because nobody's interested. Sorry.

- Don't advertise unless the forum rules say you're allowed to.

- Don't break copyright laws by posting songs, stories, photos, or other material you didn't create unless you have the creator's permission.

- Do give credit where it's due. If you do post something created by someone else, including another forum member, make sure you give them credit.

- Don't type everything in capital letters. IT'S LIKE SHOUTING.

- Don't impersonate other people or otherwise misrepresent who you are. It's okay to be anonymous (where the forum guidelines allow), but not to claim you're someone or something you aren't.

- Be relevant. Don't veer onto a completely different topic from the one under discussion. If you want to change the subject, start a new discussion.

To summarise: remember you're posting in public and your messages reflect on you personally. On the Internet, your reputation is everything so don't do anything that might tarnish it. If in doubt, leave it out.

It might seem a bit daunting to see so many rules so early on, but they pretty much cover all the taboos for all the social networking sites we'll be exploring together.

Sending emotions over the Internet

All too often, when people send text communications they can seem sterile and lack the subtlety of conversation, and this can lead to misunderstandings, particularly when you're communicating with people you don't know well. Even on the phone, you can usually tell if somebody's being sarcastic, or if they're happy or sad about something. When all you're looking at is raw words, it can be hard to define how their writer feels about them.

If you find yourself getting worked up about something you've read, take a step back and ask yourself whether it's possible that you've misunderstood what the writer intended to say, or their attitude towards it.

Not surprisingly, a whole language has emerged online to convey emotions concisely. Here's a short summary of some of the most common symbols and abbreviations you might encounter, across all the different social networking sites and discussion forums that you visit:

Conveying emotions online

Symbol or abbreviation	What it means
:-)	A smiley (tilt your head to the left and look at it). Used to indicate a smile, happiness, or joy
:-(	Feeling sad, unhappy
;-)	A wink
:-P	Sticking his/her tongue out
LOL	Laughing out loud. Used to mean something's funny. Most people probably aren't actually laughing aloud, though
ROFL or ROTFL	Rolling on the floor laughing. Again, a mild exaggeration of how funny something really is
OMG	An exclamation of shock – taken from "Oh my God!"
WTH	What the hell! You might also see WTF, but hopefully won't want to use it
IMO or IMHO	In my (humble) opinion
SMH	Shaking my head

If it helps to make your meaning clearer, you can use these abbreviations. Sometimes tacking a smiley onto the end of a message can defuse a potentially incendiary reaction in people, if they otherwise would have thought you were serious.

Don't assume everybody knows what all these abbreviations mean. Smileys and LOL are pretty safe to use everywhere. Anything else might not be fully understood.

More abbreviations for chat rooms and forums

To help save your time and effort typing lengthy messages, there are also abbreviations that are used purely for brevity, rather than to convey any emotion. Look out for the following.

More abbreviations seen in forums and chat rooms

Abbreviation	What it means
A/S/L	Age/sex/location
AFAIK	As far as I know
brb	Be right back
BTW	By the way
FWIW	For what it's worth
FYI	For your information
IANAL	I am not a lawyer
IRL	In real life (i.e., off the Internet)
L8r	See you later! (goodbye!)
NSFW	Not safe for work (warning of potentially offensive content)
TTFN	Ta ta for now!
WRT	With regard/respect to

If you come across any others you're not sure about, use **www.google.com** to search for a definition, or ask somebody in the discussion.

Summary

- Social networks will walk you through the registration process when you join

- You'll need to prove that you're a real person, and will need to validate your email address

- Protect your data with a secure but memorable password

- Your profile is a snapshot of who you are

- For your profile, use a clear photo so that your friends will recognise you easily

- Many social networks can log into your webmail and collect your contact details from there automatically

- When you finish at a network, log out to stop others using your account

- The netiquette guidelines set the standard for good manners online

- Use smileys to convey your emotions in ambiguous written communications, but avoid using abbreviations that people might not understand

Brain training

Let's see how well you've taken in the basics about social networking with a quick revision quiz. There might be more than one correct answer to some of these questions, so don't be too eager to choose your final answer!

1. A good profile photo might be . . .

a) A picture of a banana, because everyone knows you love bananas

b) A photograph of you cycling over the horizon

c) A head and shoulders photo of you smiling

d) A picture of your big toe

2. Typing in all capitals is good for . . .

a) Emphasising something important you want to say

b) Showing something's supposed to be funny

c) Annoying everybody

d) Showing what you're writing is important

3. Passwords should ideally . . .

a) Be the name of your dog

b) Be in the dictionary

c) Include letters and numbers

d) Be easy to remember

4. If someone in a discussion group says Bill Gates is on the cover of the *Sergeant Pepper* album, it's okay to . . .

a) Call them a dipstick

b) Upload the sleeve so they can see he isn't

c) Point out he was only 11 years old when it came out

d) Report them for extreme stupidity

5. If somebody writes something funny you can respond with . . .

a) :-)

b) brb

c) LOL

d) IANAL

Answers

Q1 – c   **Q2** – c   **Q3** – c and d   **Q4** – c
Q5 – a and c

PART II
Connecting with friends old and new

I met up with Geoffrey again through Friends Reunited. It's amazing how little he's changed since our schooldays!

Getting in touch with friends old and new on Facebook

3

Equipment needed: Access to a computer (desktop or laptop) with an Internet connection and web browser (see Chapter 1), plus your own email address.

Skills needed: Ability to use a web browser (see Appendix A); understanding of how to register and create your profile (see Chapter 2).

In Part I, you learnt some of the tools and techniques required for exploring social networking sites. Now it is time to take a look at a few such sites, and put your skills to good use.

Facebook is the ideal place to begin your exploration of social networking for a few reasons. Firstly, it's big. Huge, in fact. With 300 million active members (people who returned to the site in the last month), Facebook has a larger population than nearly all the countries in the world. Only China, India and the USA have more citizens. It's bigger than the UK, France, Germany, South Africa, and Canada combined. That means you're certain to find friends and family already on the site that you can connect with. Facebook is the most popular social networking site, with research from the online intelligence service Hitwise showing the only website that's more popular in the UK is Google.

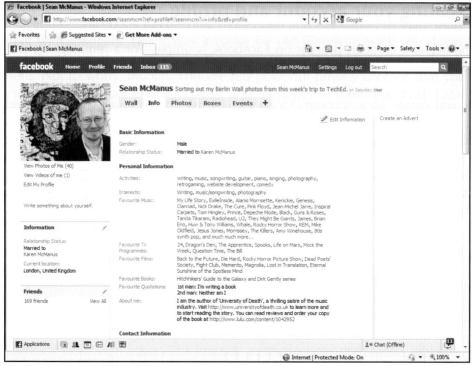

Reproduced by permission of Facebook

Figure 3.1

At the stage where your Facebook profile asks who you're 'interested in' – male or female – they are actually asking which gender you'd be interested in dating, although they missed the word 'dating' off the end. This isn't particularly obvious so tick one or the other box, unless you're happy to date both!

Looking up your friends on Facebook

After you have registered your account and created your profile, it's time to start making friends. In social networking terms, 'friend' has a slightly different meaning to that in real life. Online, a friend is just somebody you're connected to. It doesn't necessarily mean you can count on each other, sink a beer together, or even that you have ever met. Once you're connected, you might not even interact much. Facebook keeps you updated on what your friends are doing, and for some people you don't know very well, that can be enough to satisfy your curiosity. The average person on Facebook has 120 friends.

On Facebook, friends are supposed to be people that you already know from the real world. In practice, people often add others that they only know from other forums, or even people that they meet through Facebook groups.

It's up to you to decide how you want to use Facebook. When I started out, I had the guideline that I'd only have people on my friends list that I would be happy to invite to a party at my house. Later on, I broadened my guideline out, so that I'm now friends with lots of people who are just 'online friends', people I will probably only ever interact with on Facebook.

Friends can see each others' profiles, send each other messages, play games together, and take part in many of the site's other activities. On Facebook, you can only be friends with somebody if both of you agree to that relationship.

Finding friends from school and university

If you've included your places of education and work in your profile, finding your first friends will be easy. View your profile (click on the Info tab underneath your name), scroll down and you'll see links for your educational institutions and graduation years underneath the heading 'Education and Work'.

When you click on one of these links, Facebook will show you everybody who shares your institution and class year. For universities, this might be a little overwhelming, but for schools this is a great way to rediscover former classroom allies.

If you know somebody in the list and you can immediately recognise them, you can click on the Add as Friend link on the right of their name.

Facebook gives you the option of sending a message to somebody without adding them as a friend, if you want to say something to somebody you don't want to connect with more regularly. You can find this option underneath the Add a Friend link on the right-hand side.

If you're not sure whether you've found someone you know, you can click on their photo to see it at full size. You'll also see a list of their friends on the same page, which can be a good way of validating that you've found the right person. On this page, the Add as Friend link is at the top of the screen.

When you choose to add somebody as a friend, a window will appear on top of the one you're viewing. By default, a box will be ticked alongside Show in the News Feed feature of your Home Page – more on this below – so that you can see their updates when you log in, once they have accepted your friend request. This makes it easy for you to see what your friends have been doing, and it's best to leave it ticked.

Your next option is to add somebody to a friend list. Friend lists enable you to set different privacy settings for different groups of people, so that your family can see everything, but your work colleagues don't see the photos of you dancing at the weekend. Or vice versa, perhaps. Click on the Add to List button, and you can enter the name of a list to create a new one. This feature is optional, and you can manage your friend lists and privacy separately later.

By sending somebody a friend request, you're authorising them to look at your profile as a friend, so they can confirm they know you. If there's something you don't want them to see, you need to manage your privacy settings first. For more information, flick forward to the section in this chapter on 'Managing your privacy'. Until someone has accepted your request, you can't include or exclude them from particular content by name.

Click Add a Personal Message in the bottom left corner of the window if you'd like to send a personal introduction to go with your friend request. That's a particularly good idea if the person might not be sure where they know you from. Figure 3.2 shows what the friend request form looks like with a personal message. When you're done, click the Send Request button.

Your friend will then be emailed an invitation to confirm that you know each other, and they're happy to be connected to you on Facebook. Meanwhile, you can continue to browse the people you've discovered, and add new friends or send messages.

Reproduced by permission of Facebook

Figure 3.2

Once you've found an old friend, click the View Friends link, where available, to see who else they're connected to. You might well find they've already done the hard work of digging up your old buddies, and you can quickly send a friend request to those you know on their list!

You can use the same technique of clicking from your profile to search for others with the same home town or employer as you, although this tends to yield less complete results than the school and university searching.

As well as friend relationships, Facebook supports fan relationships. You'll sometimes come across profile pages dedicated to celebrities, chocolate bars or applications, and you'll have the chance to become a fan of these. The relationship is similar to a friend relationship, but the things you are a fan of will be listed separately on your profile.

Finding friends by name

Browsing your alumni is a good way to kick start your friends list, but there will be some people you'll have to search for by name. The Search box in the top right of the screen (see Figure 3.1) can be used to navigate to your existing friends or to find new people. As you type in a name, it will offer suggestions from your existing friend list. Choose one of those and you'll be taken to that friend's profile. If you're looking for someone new, just continue typing and then hit the Enter key or click on the magnifying glass.

The resulting search results look similar to those for your school or university, except everybody has the same name, which would have made for a rather surreal morning registration if it had happened at school. You can send friend requests using the same technique you used for classmates.

A couple that have the same name got engaged after meeting on Facebook. Kelly Katrina Hildebrandt from Florida first contacted Kelly Carl Hildebrandt from Texas to say she thought it was cool that they had the same name. According to the BBC, they have confirmed that if they have children, they will not be called Kelly.

Search on your friend's maiden name and married name if you know them both, and try alternative versions of their first name. If you knew somebody as 'Jamie', you might try searching for 'James' too, for example.

If you can remember some of your friend's friends, you could try searching for them first, and then browsing their friend lists to see if they've already connected with your friend. If your friend has a particularly common name (such as John Smith) but one of his friends doesn't (such as Zaphod Beeblebrox), search for the less common name first.

Who was the social butterfly of your class or company? Search for them and you might well find that their friends list makes it easy for you to find a lot of other people you know and want to reconnect with.

If you click Friends on the main navbar, and then click Find Friends, Facebook will suggest members that it thinks might belong on your friends list. You can click these to see a cut-down profile and send a friend request.

Receiving friend requests

It takes two to tango. Facebook won't let you become somebody's friend unless they agree that's what they want too. For every invitation, there is an equal and opposite confirmation.

Let's look at how you manage your friend requests. It'll give you some insight into what's going on behind the scenes after you've invited people to connect with you right now, and will prepare you for when your own requests start flooding in.

If somebody adds you as a friend, you'll receive a rather plain-looking email from Facebook to let you know. You can click on the link in that email to go to your friend requests page. You can also find a link to your friend requests on the right-hand side of your Home Page (see Figure 3.3).

Facebook is tactful: it won't let any of its members suffer outright rejection. So your options are to confirm the friendship, or to ignore the request. If you ignore the request, it'll just go away. The person who sent it won't know whether you received it and decided you can't stand the sight of them, whether it never got through, or whether it's still awaiting your judgement. Ignorance is better than insult, the logic goes.

There's also an easy link to send a message to someone if you'd like to reply without confirming the friendship. You could use this for messages like: "Hmmmm. Your face looks familiar . . . Remind me, where do I know you from?"

Interacting with your friends on Facebook

After all the work that goes in to finding friends and creating your profile, it's time for the real fun to begin. Facebook makes it easy to keep in touch with your friends in lots of different ways, which we'll explore now.

Viewing your News Feed

When you log in to Facebook, or you click on the Home link on the blue navbar at the top of the screen, you'll be taken to your *News Feed* section. These news bulletins highlight what your friends have been doing on the site, including announcing their success (or otherwise) in various games, any photos they've uploaded, and what's on their mind (if they typed it in – the site's clever, but not *that* clever!). The updates are sorted by time, with the latest ones higher up on the screen, as you can see in Figure 3.3.

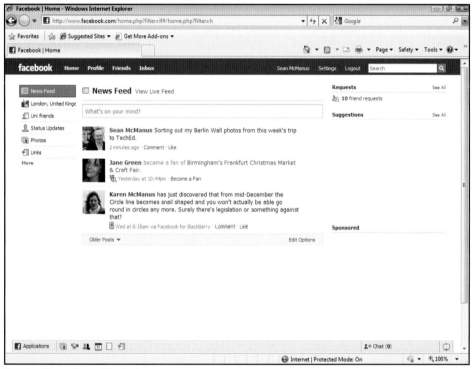

Reproduced by permission of Facebook

Figure 3.3

After reading your friend's news you might like to get straight on with sending them a response. To do so, click the Comment link underneath an update, and you'll see a larger box appear for you to type your response into. When you click Comment, your response is attached to that news update wherever it is shown. That means everybody who sees your friend's update in their News Feed also sees your comment along with it. When others add their comments, you'll see those, too. In case you miss them, Facebook sends you an email to let you know if anyone added their thoughts to an update you previously commented on.

Alternatively, if you just want to encourage someone or to recognise their wit or talent, you can click on the Like link underneath their update. Facebook keeps a count of how many people like each update and anyone who can see the update can see who liked it too.

The News Feed just shows you edited highlights, as determined by Facebook. If you want to see everything that people have been doing on the site, click the Live Feed link at the top of your News Feed. If you want to see everything that people have been doing on the site, click the Live Feed link at the top of your News Feed. Click the News Feed link when you want the short version again. Many people prefer the Live Feed and you should review it to see what you're missing, and then decide which version you prefer.

Pruning the News Feed

You might find all the Facebook updates a bit overwhelming at first, particularly if you've got friends who seem to spend all day on there clogging up your News Feed. You can stay friends with them but hide their updates, so they don't appear on your Home Page. Don't worry about offending them – they'll never know!

To do this, go to any update and hover over it. On the right-hand side, you'll see a Hide link appear. If you click that, you'll see a menu appear with the option to hide that person. When you click the Hide [name] link, all their updates disappear from your Home Page. Note that their comments on other people's updates remain.

If you want to give someone a second chance, you can unhide them. Scroll to the bottom of your News Feed, and you'll see a link to Edit Options so you can bring people back again.

From time to time, games sweep Facebook and your News Feed can get clogged up with 'animal husbandry' news from make-believe farms and 'high score' updates from puzzle games. You can hide these games in the same way as you hide people. To recover them, click Edit Options and then click Applications.

Grouping your friends

You can organise your friends into lists so that you can group updates from school friends, work colleagues and family in separate places. That means you can choose to check in with family more often than friends, and can more easily get an overview of what particular groups are up to. The lists help you to manage your privacy too, because you can control which lists have access to which information from your profile.

Facebook sometimes creates lists for you automatically, so you might find you already have a list for family members and for any companies you've worked at or hobby groups you belong to.

To create your own lists, click Friends on the main blue navbar. On the left-hand side, you'll see a Lists section. By default, everybody is in your Friends list. Click the Create link underneath your lists, and you can begin to build a new list.

On the Friend Browser, shown in Figure 3.4, click on anyone you'd like to add to your list and Facebook highlights them in blue.

Reproduced by permission of Facebook

Figure 3.4

Above the Cancel button you will see some numbers. These are links that take you through your (one or more) pages of friends. If you click on the number 3, you'll jump to the third page, for example. Clicking on Next takes you to the next page in the sequence. Even though you can't see your friends on the first page any more, they'll remain selected. In the top left, there's a counter that shows how many friends you've selected, so you can make sure you haven't lost any along the way.

If there's someone specific you want to add to the list, type their name into the box on the right, select them, and then clear that text box again to get the full list back. Don't forget to give your list a short name by entering it into the box at the top left. When you've finished, click the Create New List button.

Once you have created a list, it appears in your lists on the left-hand navbar. When in the Friends area, you can click your list name to see who's a member of it, add or remove members, or delete the whole list.

The lists are just for your use, so don't worry about where you put people because they'll never find out. You can add people to multiple lists too, so they might appear in both school friends and best friends, for example.

When you return to your News Feed, you'll see that the lists you've created have been added to your left-hand navbar. You can see my Uni Friends list in Figure 3.3. If you don't see a particular list, try clicking the More link at the bottom of the navbar. When you click a list name, Facebook filters your Home Page to show only the updates from the people in that list. If you want to see everybody again, click News Feed at the top of the navbar (highlighted blue in Figure 3.3).

You also have the option to add people to lists when you invite them to be a friend or confirm a friend invitation, so that it's easy to keep your lists up to date.

Sharing what you're doing

So you've just discovered how to look at what your friends have been up to, but how do you tell them about your own activities? Easy! At the top of your News Feed page, you'll see a What's on your mind? form box, as shown in Figure 3.3. Facebook calls this box your Publisher and it can be used to share what you're

in Facebook-speak). You can also customise the settings to make pictures available to (or hidden from) different individuals and lists of friends.

3. If you're using Internet Explorer and this is your first album upload, you need to confirm that you authorise the photo upload software. Click on the yellow line at the top of the website window and then select Install This Add-on For All Users of This Computer.

4. If you're using Windows Vista and this is your first album upload, you need to click the button to confirm you want to install this software.

5. Once it's installed, the photo uploader shows your computer folders on the left. Click the folders to find where your photos are stored. All the photos in a chosen folder are shown on the right, as shown in Figure 3.6. Use the Scroll bar on the right of the box if the photos don't all fit on the screen at once.

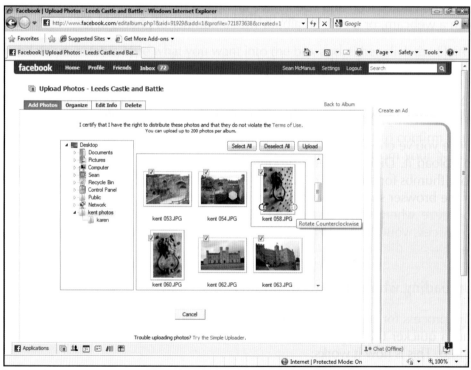

Figure 3.6

6. Tick the box on each photo you'd like to upload. There's a Select All button to automate the process if you want to upload everything. If you want to

share nearly all the photos, it's quicker to select them all using the button and then untick the ones you don't want.

7. When you hover over a photo, you can rotate it left or right by clicking the controls that appear in the bottom corners. In Figure 3.6 I'm hovering over the third photo, to show you the controls.

8. As it uploads, Facebook shows you a progress bar with a sneak preview of what it's uploading.

If you can't get the software to install, there is a simple uploader you can use, and Facebook provides links to it on most of the album upload pages. The simple uploader requires you to browse for each photo individually, and can only upload five at a time. Photo uploading is much quicker using the add-on, so you should use it if you can.

After your photos have been uploaded, you'll have a chance to add captions to each one. This is an optional step, but it can help your friends understand what they're looking at. You can also pick one photo to be the album cover, which is what people see when browsing all your albums.

If you make any changes after uploading your photos, make sure you scroll down to click the Save Changes button at the bottom of the album upload page.

The Organize tab at the top of your album lets you change the order of the photos, and the Edit Info tab enables you to change the album's title and the description of its contents. If you want to add new photos, click Add More.

You can get to your albums at any time through your profile, using the main navbar to get there and then clicking the Photos tab (as shown in Figure 3.1). When you go into your albums, you'll see the same publishing, editing, captioning, tagging, adding, and deletion options that you had when you uploaded them. Any photos you upload individually are automatically added to your wall photos album.

Your new album doesn't become available to your friends until you publish it. To do that, you click the Publish Now button at the top of the screen when you're editing the album.

Any time you're asked if you want to publish your album while you're still editing it, you can safely click the Skip button and your photos will remain on the site, but visible only to you.

Before you publish your album, though, let me tell you about a neat feature that your friends will love or hate you for, depending on what's in your photos!

Tagging people in photos

Of course, what people most want to know about your photos is whether they are in them or not. To label someone in a picture, you need to tag them, in Facebook jargon. This basically means that you say where they are in the photo, and what their name is. Facebook then sends a message to tell your friends that they've been tagged, so they can view the photo and leave comments on it. Photos can also be seen by the friends of those who have been tagged, and become accessible through the profile of the person you tagged.

You need to take care with tagging. Because of the way it draws attention to who is in a photo, it's a bit like passing the prints among the friends of whoever's in the photo. Clearly, you wouldn't want to upload anything compromising anyway, but tags should sometimes be omitted for more subtle reasons. Younger relatives might not want all their school friends to see pictures of them boogie-ing with granny at a family party, for example.

Before you publish your album, you can add a tag to any of the people pictures, including any of yourself. Just click on the face of the person you'd like to tag. You'll see a box open up with the names of your friends in it, and you can tick them to tag them. You can tag multiple people in the same photo, if it's a group shot.

When you tag somebody, the photo is published immediately, even if the album it's in hasn't been published yet.

It's not just your own photos you can tag. When you're viewing your friends' photos, there's a Tag This Photo link underneath them, so you can add yourself or others to those too.

Sharing videos

The process for sharing a video is the same as for sharing a single photo. Just use the icon of a video camera and follow the instructions on the screen. Videos take a long time to upload, and it might look like nothing's happening, but have faith. It will work (usually).

Once it's uploaded, you'll have a chance to add a title and description and to tag who is in the film. The privacy controls allow you to control who has access to the video, and you can pick a representative thumbnail picture from a selection of frames Facebook has lifted from your film.

You can find all your videos by going to your profile and then clicking See All in the videos section on the left.

Sharing links

If you see something online you'd like to share, Facebook makes it easy. To share a link, write your note about it in the Publisher box as usual, and then click the icon of a note pinned to a board. You'll be prompted to enter the website address. Facebook then makes a short summary of the website and takes some pictures from it, so that you don't have to provide much explanation. You can use the left and right arrows to click through the pictures and choose one to represent the web page.

If you want to copy and paste the website address from another browser window, click it and hold down the Control key on the keyboard while you tap the A key. The address should now be highlighted. Then hold down the Control key and tap the C key. Click in the Facebook Publisher box for the website address, and then hold down the Control key and tap the V key. The website address should now be copied across without you having to retype it.

Visiting a friend's profile

To visit a friend's profile, you can click their name or picture against any of their entries or comments in your News Feed. You can also click them in your friends list, or search for them by name using the Search box on the top right of the screen.

Your friend's profile will look much like yours. There are four tabs across the top of it:

- **Wall:** This is a message board that will include their latest activities on the site. There's a box at the top of this which works exactly like your Publisher, except that any message you write here appears on your friend's profile as well as your own. When you go to a friend's profile, this is where you will arrive.

- **Info:** This is where you get to find out that your friend is a closet Bay City Rollers fan! As well as their interests and professional details, you can find contact details here.

- **Photos:** This shows you all photos either featuring your friend, or uploaded by him or her. You can comment on any of the photos, and add tags if there are others in the photos you'd like to label.

- **Boxes:** This includes different applications they've installed. We'll talk more about applications later in this chapter, but it's often worth taking a look to see what else they've discovered Facebook can do!

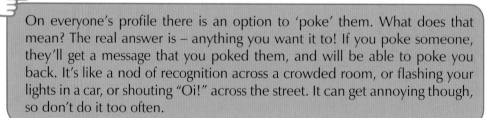

On everyone's profile there is an option to 'poke' them. What does that mean? The real answer is – anything you want it to! If you poke someone, they'll get a message that you poked them, and will be able to poke you back. It's like a nod of recognition across a crowded room, or flashing your lights in a car, or shouting "Oi!" across the street. It can get annoying though, so don't do it too often.

If you have an attack of l'esprit d'escalier and think of a witty retort too late, you can dig into the archive to find recent posts by your friends. Type

continued

your keywords into the Search box at the top right of the screen, and then choose Posts by Friends in the menu on the left (as shown in Figure 3.10 later). You can find the post without having to trawl through pages of profile and then leave your sparkling comment. Better late than never.

Sending a private message

While a lot of the interaction on Facebook does take place in public, you can also send a private message to a friend. This is ideal for the kinds of messages that won't be of interest to anyone else, such as when you're meeting up at the pub.

To send a private message, you just visit your friend's profile and click the Send a Message link underneath their profile picture.

A communication sent using the messaging feature in a social network is as private as an email. Email itself shouldn't be considered much more private than a postcard, though: it's possible for emails to be intercepted and read in transit, as they bounce from server to server to traverse the Internet. It's also possible that somebody else could access the email account on the other end, similar to the way that a letter could be opened by somebody else. In reality, messages are highly unlikely to be read by anyone other than the intended recipient, but it's good practice not to put anything in them that you wouldn't want published. That includes, at the very least, credit card and banking information.

The messages you receive are kept in your Inbox on the site, which you can find through the main blue navbar at the top of the screen. When you receive a message or a reply, Facebook sends you the message by email and a link to it in your Inbox so you can reply to it on Facebook.

Facebook organises messages by conversation, so you can see what was said previously as part of the same sequence of to-and-fro messages. At the end of the message thread, as this organised list is known, you'll find a box so you can easily reply. Figure 3.7 shows an example message thread.

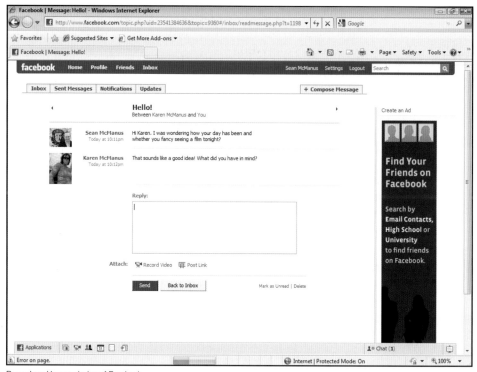

Figure 3.7

You can send a private message to more than one person at a time. Just add multiple names or friend lists in the To: field when you're creating your message.

Chatting with friends online in real time

Whereas private messages are like sending a letter, chatting online is more like making a phone call. Both parties are there at the same time, and messages are read as soon as they're sent. That results in more conversational communication, because people can respond to each other straight away. If you've used instant messaging online, with programs like Windows Messenger or AOL Instant Messenger, then this idea will already be familiar to you – the chat integrated in Facebook is similar.

There are a couple of advantages to using Facebook chat. Firstly, there's no software to install. That means you can get started straight away and can chat from anywhere you can access the Web.

The second advantage of using Facebook is that you can keep in touch with all your friends, without having to find out or remember separate chat IDs. If you're friends with someone on Facebook, you're set.

At the bottom of the screen, you'll have noticed a grey bar that Facebook's added (see Figure 3.7). Even when you scroll the page, that bar stays on screen. On the right-hand side, there's a Chat link. If you click that, you'll see a menu open up, showing which of your friends are available to chat. Those with a green spot next to them are online now. Anybody with a greyed-out spot was online recently, and you could try chatting to see if they're still there. Facebook describes these people as idle, which seems a bit harsh.

Click on somebody you want to chat with, and you'll see a new window open up with your friend's name and profile picture at the top of it. At the bottom is a one-line box where you can type a message. You can write as much as you like in this box; it doesn't have to fit into the space there. It's good practice to limit what you write to a couple of sentences though.

When you press the Enter key, your message is sent to your friend, and appears in the Chat box. Your friend can then write a reply. You can tell when your friend is typing, because a speech bubble appears next to their name at the bottom of the chat window, as shown in Figure 3.8.

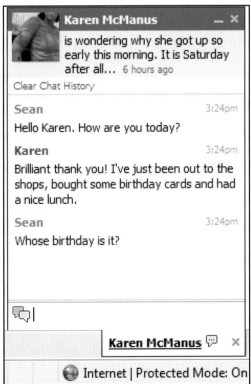

Reproduced by permission of Facebook

Figure 3.8

You can click the Minimise icon at the top right of the chat window (the small horizontal line) to hide it. That won't do anything to stop your conversation, and you can even browse around the Facebook site while chatting. If somebody sends you a chat message while the window's minimised, you'll see a red speech bubble flash up.

You can have different chat conversations going on at the same time. You can only have one chat window visible at once, though, with the rest minimised. You'll be alerted by a red speech bubble when there's something to respond to in a particular chat window. Each chat can have only two people in it.

If you don't want to be disturbed by chat invitations, you can click on the Chat menu at the bottom right of the screen, click Options and then select Go Offline at the top of that menu. Your friends won't be able to see that you're on Facebook then and won't be able to initiate any chats with you. You'll go back online automatically when you next click the Chat menu.

Challenging your friends to a game on Facebook

Facebook applications are additional features that you can plug in to the site. Typically, they're games, but you can also find applications that help you track where you've travelled to, share book reviews, display horoscopes, share slideshows, and keep track of birthdays and social engagements. There are also applications that can help you to integrate Facebook with other social networks, including Twitter, which I cover in Chapter 5.

The privacy implications of using applications

The strength of applications is that they can use your personal information on Facebook to enhance your experience. Games can use your profile photo to represent you in the game, or look at your friends list so they can show you how your scores compare with other players you know. The caveat is that in order to do this, applications need access to your Facebook profile and the information stored in it.

 Facebook requires the developers of applications to sign up to its terms and conditions, which say they must delete any personal information they acquire after 24 hours. But anybody can be a Facebook developer, and most applications aren't vetted. You don't always know who you're giving your profile information to when you install an application.

Mostly, the issue of access doesn't matter too much: you probably shouldn't be sharing anything in Facebook that would cause you problems if it leaked. There are ways in which you can check the reputation of an application too, so you can minimise the risk.

Finding and installing applications

At the bottom left of the screen, you'll see an Applications link. Click that, and then choose Browse More Applications from the menu. You'll arrive at the application directory, where you can find all the applications you can add to your profile.

The Featured by Facebook section highlights some of the best applications, and underneath is the full list of applications. Use the triangle buttons on the right side of the blue header stripe for each section, and you can skip through the pages of results.

 You can enter a keyword related to one of your hobbies in the Search box on the left to find related applications. You can also browse the applications in different categories, including business, education and sports, using the links on the left-hand side. When you go into a category, you can use the pull-down menu above the Featured by Facebook box on the right-hand side. This enables you to filter applications by subcategory, such as 'dating' under lifestyle and 'word games' under games.

Any applications that are in the Featured by Facebook box or have a green tick beside their five-star rating have been verified by Facebook. That means they have passed Facebook's own standards for offering a trustworthy user experience. I recommend you restrict yourself to using verified applications, at least until you get to grips with applications properly.

When you click an application, you'll arrive at its info page. This looks a bit like a Facebook profile and includes a small summary of the application, details of which of your friends use it, the size of the user base (how many people use it altogether) and how many reviews it's had, as well as the average score of those reviews. You can click the link for the number of reviews to read a selection of them. Look for the badge on the left-hand side that shows the application has been verified by Facebook.

If you decide to install an application, click the Go to Application button on the left-hand side of the screen. When you do that, Facebook warns you that you're sharing your personal information with this application.

Click the Allow button, and your application is installed. From here on, every application is different and it's not possible to talk you through all of them. You will probably find those that are verified by Facebook provide an intuitive enough experience that you can work out how to get started.

If you install an application that you want to get rid of again, you can do that by choosing Edit Applications from the applications pop-up menu on the bottom left of the screen. It shows you a list of all your applications, and you can click on the X to remove any that you don't want any more. When you remove an application, all traces of it will be deleted from your profile.

Since it's easy enough to delete applications, there's no harm in trying some out to see which ones you like.

To run an application you've installed, you usually select it from the applications pop-up menu at the bottom left of the screen. When you find an application you love, you can create a shortcut so you can get to it in a single click. While you're using the application, click the link that says Bookmark [application name] on the grey bar across the bottom of the screen. This adds a button to that grey stripe so you can jump straight to the application or game in future.

Playing games on Facebook

There are all kinds of games and quizzes on Facebook. You've probably seen a few as you've been browsing other people's profiles: personality and general knowledge quizzes are particularly popular. You can usually start using these quizzes by clicking on your friends' results in their profile pages.

 When playing quizzes, pay attention so you don't get confused by the advertising. The quiz operators are often paid for the number of people who click on the adverts, so they'll sometimes make the adverts look like a feature of the quiz.

Facebook also hosts some more sophisticated games. Bowling Buddies enables you to play at 10-pin bowling and challenge your friends to a game. The application is verified by Facebook and has over two million users, so you might well find some of your friends are already players.

Install the game using the instructions above, and then click on the Practice link to start playing.

To pick up the bowling ball, you click and hold the mouse. You then push your mouse forward. When the ball crosses the line marked near the start of the lane, it'll be dropped into play. Whether the ball hits the skittles or not depends on how fast you push the mouse forward and how straight you push it. Your score will be shared with your friends, so make sure you limber up before you pick up the mouse. As Figure 3.9 shows, it's harder than it sounds!

 If your computer's a bit slow, you can click on the buttons that say 3D and Fast PC to make the interface simpler and speed things up.

Figure 3.9

When you finish a game, Bowling Buddies will show you how you rank compared with your friends who have played. If you want to challenge someone directly, click on the Challenge button on the game's main menu. You'll be asked to pick one of your friends, and will then play a game as usual. At the end, your friend will be invited to play their side of the game next time they start Bowling Buddies. Facebook will notify you once they've played and will tell you what the result was.

The score table underneath the main game window will show you how many games you've won, and your highest score, and will show those of your friends too.

Bowling Buddies is just one of hundreds of arcade games that are available on Facebook; there are also word games, board games (including Bingo and Chess), card games, role-playing games, and so on. Why not see what you can find?

Finding interest groups

As well as helping you to keep in touch with people you know in the real world, Facebook provides a place for you to discuss your interests with both friends and strangers. Groups host discussion boards and shared photo albums, and have their own walls on which you can post comments and links too.

To find relevant groups, just type your interest into the Search box and press Enter. You can also visit your profile and click on one of your interests or hobbies to search the site for people and groups related to it.

Click on Groups in the left navbar on the search results screen, and you can see relevant groups arranged with the largest ones at the top, as shown in Figure 3.10.

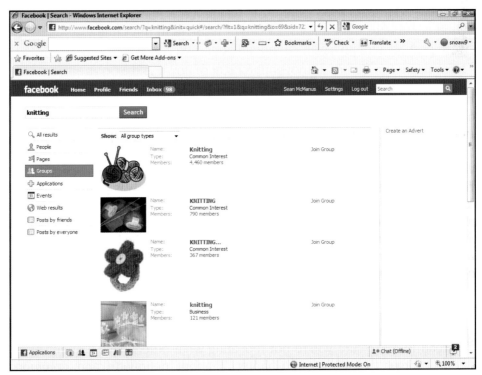

Reproduced by permission of Facebook

Figure 3.10

Click on the group's name and you can usually view its member list, wall and discussion boards to see whether you'd like to join.

Figure 3.12 shows the profile privacy page.

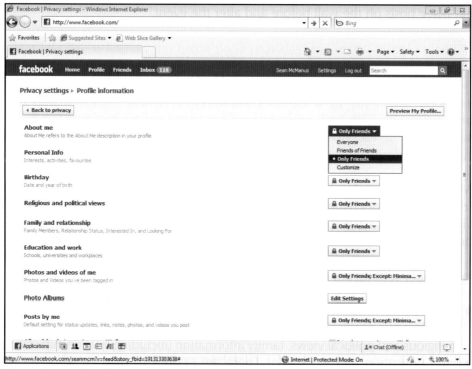

Reproduced by permission of Facebook

Figure 3.12

For each element of your profile, you can choose an appropriate privacy setting, using a pull-down menu. Figure 3.12 shows the menu open for the About Me section. I've restricted my information to my friends here. You might prefer to extend access beyond your friends to their friends (friends of friends) or to everyone, which makes the information public on the Internet.

Your name, profile picture, gender, current city, and friend list are always considered public information and are available to everyone, although you can hide yourself from search results.

For each element of your profile, there is also an option to customise the settings, enabling you to make content available to specific friends, or to hide it from specific friends. You can use friend lists in place of the names of friends, which makes this feature particularly powerful. You could provide different access to friends and family, for example, or to work friends and school friends. These settings can be different for each section of your profile too, so that work colleagues might see your educational background but not your political views, while for family it might be the other way around. You can also limit the view to yourself only using these settings, effectively hiding that part of your profile from everyone else. Figure 3.13 shows the privacy settings for one of my profile elements.

Custom privacy

✓ **Make this visible to**

These people: Only Friends   ▼

Only friends can see this.

✗ **Hide this from**

These people: Family ✕   James Taylor ✕

Save Setting   Cancel

Reproduced by permission of Facebook

Figure 3.13

The main privacy settings page also enables you to block specific people from having any contact with you or any access to your information. You're unlikely to ever need this feature, but it is there in case somebody is spoiling your Facebook experience and you can't resolve the issue any other way. Don't forget you can hide their updates on your News Feed, so they virtually disappear but you remain able to contact one another.

As you tinker with your profile's settings, you can preview it through the eyes of one of your friends. Click the Preview My Profile button at the top of your profile privacy settings page (see Figure 3.12) and you can enter a friend's name to see exactly what they will see under your current settings.

Speeding up Facebook

If your computer is getting on a bit and Facebook seems slow, there is a way to speed it up. Facebook Lite is a cut-down version of the site that is optimised for speed.

The price you pay is that you can't do everything you can with the full version of Facebook. Applications and groups are the main omissions, and the Facebook Lite search focuses purely on people.

You can carry out the most common activities, though. What Facebook Lite enables you to do is update your status, publish photos and videos, read status updates, comment, accept friend requests, write on other people's walls and look at your friends' photos. To give Facebook Lite a go, visit **www.lite.facebook.com**.

Ahoy there! Click the English link at the bottom of the screen and you can change your language to English (pirate). Your friends become 'me hearties', your Home Page is now your 'home port', and you update your status by answering "what be troublin' ye?" Among the 70 language choices, you can also find Irish, Welsh and Esperanto, and the mind-melting English with an upside-down alphabet.

Summary

- Facebook has a vast membership and sophisticated privacy controls, making a good choice for your first social network

- You can only be friends with someone on Facebook if you both agree

- If you don't want to be friends with someone, ignore their request. Facebook won't tell them

- Your News Feed shows you what your friends have been doing on Facebook

- You can use Facebook to publish status updates, photos, videos, links and events. Friends can see them in their News Feeds and comment on them

- If you tag people in photos or status updates, they'll be notified that you included them in your content

- If you write on a friend's wall, your message will be visible on their profile. Send a message or chat to communicate privately

- Applications enable you to play games, but carry privacy implications

- Join groups to discuss your interests with other Facebook members, including those you do not already know

- Your privacy settings enable you to restrict access to different parts of your profile. Friends lists help you to give different permissions to friends and family

- If your computer runs slowly, try using Facebook Lite

Brain training

Are you now an expert on Facebook? Put your grey matter to the test with this quiz. There might be more than one correct answer to some of these questions.

1. Facebook is open to . . .

a) Students

b) People in the USA

c) Only people who are invited to join

d) Anybody, of any age, anywhere in the world

2. You can find friends on Facebook by . . .

a) Searching by name

b) Browsing people by school or college

c) Checking who Facebook suggests you befriend

d) Looking at your friends' friends

3. Your Publisher box can be used to share . . .

a) Links to interesting stories you've found online

b) Holiday photos

c) Videos

d) News of what you're doing

e) Fairy cakes

4. Your News Feed will show you . . .

a) The latest headlines from the BBC

b) What your friends have been doing on Facebook

c) What you've been doing on Facebook

d) The latest business developments at Facebook

5. If you write on a friend's wall . . .

a) You'll leave crayon on their wallpaper

b) You'll send them a private message

c) You'll add a message to their public profile

d) You'll break the rules of Facebook

Answers

Q1 – d   **Q2** – All four are correct!   **Q3** – a, b, c and d

Q4 – b and c   **Q5** – c

Finding old schoolmates at Friends Reunited

4

Equipment needed: Access to a computer (desktop or laptop) with an Internet connection and web browser (see Chapter 1), plus your own email address.

Skills needed: Ability to use a web browser (see Appendix A); understanding of how to register and create your profile (see Chapter 2).

Friends Reunited (**www.friendsreunited.co.uk**) has a bold ambition: to have everybody in the UK registered, so that old friends never lose touch. So far, it's recruited over half the UK's adult population, with 20.6 million registered members. The site attracts adults of all ages, with the average age of users 42, and 11 million users over 35.

Of all the sites you'll be looking at in this book, Friends Reunited is the oldest. The site began in 1999 when Steve and Julie Pankhurst started to develop a website that would help people to find out what their school friends are up to today.

The site has expanded considerably since its initial focus on schools, and now helps members to reconnect with people from work, the armed forces, teams and clubs, and streets they used to live on. The schools index also recognises Australia, New Zealand, seven Southern Africa nations, three countries in Asia, and six in the Pacific Region. Adoption overseas is relatively high in South Africa (49,000 members), Singapore (31,000), and Malaysia (15,000).

In the early days, Friends Reunited charged members a subscription fee if they wanted to be able to send messages to friends. That's been abolished, so it's now free to connect with your old mates, as it is on most other social networking websites.

If you tried Friends Reunited years ago, it's worth giving it a second look now. A lot of the innovations from other social networking sites have been adopted, such as friend relationships and more in-depth profiles. Because the site's original purpose was to reconnect school colleagues and because it was so ahead of the game in social networking, it remains the best way to track down former school colleagues. There is significant cross-over between social networking sites, but there are likely to be many people on Friends Reunited that you can't find as easily elsewhere. The built-in features for organising a class reunion make it ideal for that purpose, too.

How Friends Reunited helped Pam organise her school reunion

Friends Reunited played an important role in helping Pam Fitchett (née Rutherford) to organise her school reunion. After she left Shelton Lock Secondary Modern school in 1959, she lost touch with her school friends, some of whom she'd been to school with through infants, juniors, and secondary school. Fifty years later, she reunited over 100 of them at the Allenton Royal British Legion Club.

"My kids gave me a second hand PC five years ago," she says. "That's when I started. There was a fella who went to the same school as me and played in the band at my leaving party when I went to Australia in 1963. I had had the photo from the party for 40 years, and when I found Friends Reunited, I thought I'd see if he was on there. He wasn't, but I found another fella who was also in a band and came from my school, who I didn't know. I wrote and asked him if he knew the other lad, and he was good friends with him, so I got in touch."

When this old friend, now living in Ontario, decided to take a holiday in England with his wife, Pam took the opportunity to organise a reunion. "Another old girlfriend came from New Jersey in America," she says. "These were all people

I hadn't seen since I was at school, and we're all 65 years old now. We were petrified; all anxious. It was like being 14 or 15 again. But it was absolutely amazing. We didn't have any music – we just spent the night talking. One person brought an 8mm film from a school trip. It was funny how the old groups that used to stick together at school did that at the reunion too."

Pam is now in touch with four teachers and 150 former pupils from her old school, made up of about half of her year of 200 pupils, and others from different years. Half of those people she tracked down by sending direct messages through Friends Reunited. "I always look each week to see if any new members have joined," Pam says. "I write straight away if I find anyone new. Some people get the dates a little wrong, so I also check the year above or below mine."

"It was very difficult to find the girls," she says. "They get married and change their names. So I started writing to lads with the same surnames, hoping they were the brothers of the girls or some relation."

Pam also used online directory services sites and Facebook to track people down. "They call me Miss Marple," she jokes. "If someone's lost contact with a friend, they call me. 'Ask Pam, she'll find them,' they say. I'm so happy if I can put people back in touch again."

Facebook is also used to share photos from the old days and the reunions. "I have about 67 friends on Facebook and I've posted about 300 photos. Every week I'm writing to people in Canada, Australia, France, Spain and all over England and I use the chat to keep in touch with people when they log on."

Now that Pam has tracked down so many of her old schoolmates, there are plans to have a big meet-up annually, as well as a monthly lunch club for those near to the school's county of Derbyshire. "One lady I met again 18 months ago was my best friend at school," says Pam. "I'm seeing her every month now and it's as if we've never been apart. Friends Reunited has made a world of difference to at least 100 odd of us. We'll never lose that friendship now."

Pam's advice to others thinking about organising a reunion? "Go for it! It's amazing to turn the clock back that many years and feel young again."

Creating your account

Registration at Friends Reunited is straightforward, but will prompt you to provide information which is shared with all site members. You'll be asked to provide some quick answers to fill out your profile, including your marital status, whether you have children, and what you do for a living. There is also an About Me box for you to write your short life story.

Although you can edit or delete this information later, you can't hide it: if it's on the site, it's available to all members. These boxes are all optional, though, so you can leave them blank if you prefer.

To update your profile at any time, hover over the navbar where it says Profile and click My Profile.

Adding your school or other place

After you've registered, Friends Reunited invites you to search for the first place you spent time at, so you can start catching up with old friends straight away. Later on, you can add other schools and places by hovering over Places on the navbar across the top of the screen, and then clicking Find a Place.

The first step is to add your primary school. Friends Reunited helps you to search for it, but you'll have to imagine you're zooming in on it from outer space. In the Search box on the left, use the pull-down menu to say what type of place you're searching for, first. Enter its name in the next box, and then help Friends Reunited to target it by choosing its country, region, and county. With each selection, a new form field will appear to help you select the next one, down to the county level as shown in Figure 4.1. When you're done, click Search.

If you can't remember what your school was called, or if it won't come up in the search results for some reason, you can browse all the schools on the site to find it. On the right, start by clicking on Primary School, and then choose your country, region, and county. The site shows you all the schools it knows in that county. There are probably thousands of them, so to save spending all day sifting through them, use the alphabet links across the top of the search results to jump to schools beginning with the same letter as your school. (If you can't

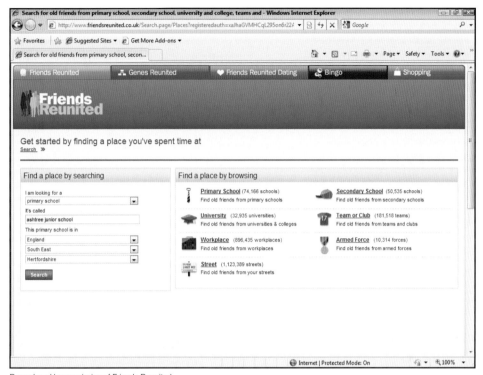

Reproduced by permission of Friends Reunited

Figure 4.1

spell your school's name well enough to know the first letter, it's probably not worth tracking it down again!) There might still be several pages of these results – so browse through the pages by clicking on the number links just above the alphabet.

Hopefully, you should now see your school shown on the right-hand side of the page, beside the Search box. Aah! The memories come flooding back!

Click its name, and you'll get a chance to join this school, as shown in Figure 4.2, only this time you don't have to polish your shoes and stand up straight. Enter your years of joining and leaving. Don't forget there's a calculator built into Windows if you need it to work out the dates (you'll find it in the Accessories folder, after you go through the Start button at the bottom left of the Windows Desktop). Click Join Now when you're ready.

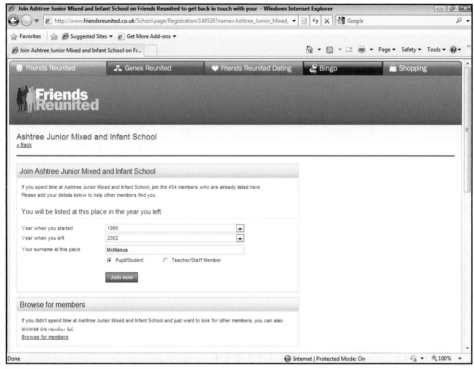

Reproduced by permission of Friends Reunited

Figure 4.2

At the bottom of the screen is a link to browse members without joining a school. You can use this to help track down friends from other schools, or to see who's already registered from your school before you join them.

Finding your former schoolmates

Once you've joined a school, Friends Reunited shows you the other people who have joined that school, starting with your leaving year. Seeing some of these names takes me back. I can almost smell the chalk and feel the wind rushing through my hair as I skid across the hall floor on my knees (sorry Mum). Figure 4.3 shows an example school page.

If there's someone in particular you'd like to find, type their first and last name into the Search box at the top of the pupil list and then press the Enter key. You

Reproduced by permission of Friends Reunited

Figure 4.3

should see only those people who went to the school you're browsing and who have that name. To bring everyone else back, clear those boxes and click on Find again.

Some people might have left your school early, and quite a few are bound to have miscalculated their leaving dates. Our maths teachers would be ashamed. You can browse a few years either side of your leaving date by clicking on the year dates at the top of the search results (shown in Figure 4.3). If you click and hold the Earlier or Later links at each side of those years, you'll see other years scroll into place from the left or right.

To find out what someone's been up to since you gave up playing marbles together, click their name in the search results to view their profile. From here, you can read the description they've written about themselves, and view any photos, videos and hobbies they want to share.

Getting back in touch with old friends

Friends Reunited gives you several options for interacting with people from their profiles, all shown in Figure 4.4.

Reproduced by permission of Friends Reunited

Figure 4.4

The most basic way is to leave what Friends Reunited calls a buzz. This feature enables you to select from one of 15 standard messages saying things like "I stopped by", "It's been too long", and "Hello!" You can also choose a picture to leave behind, including a love heart, a cake, or a waving hand.

When you select your message and click the Add Buzz button, your buzz message is added to the recipient's profile, together with your name and a link back to your profile. By default, buzzes are visible to everyone viewing the profile.

If you have more to say or want to respond to something that somebody has written in their profile, you can leave a public comment. Click the Comment tab to do this – you can then type a message up to 1,000 characters long. A countdown underneath the Comment text box shows how many characters you have left. When you click Add Comment, it immediately appears on the recipient's public profile, so make sure you only write things that you'll both be happy to see shared in public.

If you'd like to reminisce about good times behind the bike sheds, or would just like to send a more personal, friendly greeting, you can send a private mail.

Don't forget that you shouldn't use private messages to send sensitive information, such as credit card details. They are private, but they're not secure.

To send a mail, click the first tab in the Contact box (as shown in Figure 4.4). Above the text box, you should see a confirmation that the message is private and is not displayed on the profile.

Friends Reunited has some ice-breakers to help you start a conversation after all those years. Click on the Try One of our Quick Suggestions link and the ice-breakers appear underneath it. When you click an ice-breaker, it is pasted into the message box ready for you to use.

Whether you choose to leave a buzz, a comment or a mail, the person you're contacting is sent an email to tell them about your message so you don't need to worry if or when they will find it.

Registering more places

To find more people, you can add more places, starting with your secondary school and university. The steps are the same as those for adding your primary school. As well as schools and colleges, Friends Reunited recognises armed forces, teams or clubs, workplaces and streets. Registering these places can help you to find (and be found by) people who shared your later life, but who don't know what school you went to.

To get started, hover over the Places link on the navbar and select Find a Place.

You can also search Friends Reunited by name. Along the top of most screens is a Search bar, into which you can enter the first and second name you're looking for. Unless you're looking for somebody with a strikingly unusual name, this can result in a fairly long list of people, though. If you know somebody's school, you're better off searching there first to narrow the area.

> If you want to see Friends Reunited's suggestions for people you might know, select Suggested Friends from the Friends pop-up menu on the navbar.

Adding friends to your friends lists

Friends Reunited enables you to add people to your 'friends lists'. Having done this, when you log in you'll see a summary of what your friends have been up to on the site, but the greatest benefit is that friends lists help you to manage your privacy. Using friends lists, you can close much of your personal information to the browsing public, and just open it up to those you know. You can show different parts of your profile to the general public, acquaintances and friends, so that acquaintances can't see your marital status, for example, but friends can. We will look more at the issue of privacy and how to change your privacy settings later in this chapter.

Adding somebody as a friend also makes it easier for you to communicate with them. It's like adding your friends' numbers to your mobile phone's address book, so you can quickly find them.

Sending a friend request

To add a friend to your friends list, first you need to use the techniques listed previously to find your friend and view their profile. Having done this, and with your friend's details on the screen, click on the Add as Friend button underneath their profile image. A new box will open on top of the current window, which looks like Figure 4.5.

You will see that Friends Reunited gives you two separate lists: one for acquaintances and another for friends and family. The list names are just to make them easier to understand. It's okay to put friends into the acquaintance group, and people you don't know so well into the friends group. It's just a question of how much information you want to share with these people. Your privacy settings give you control over what each group sees; you can move people between lists later. Don't worry about hurting someone's feelings: these lists are only visible to you.

Reproduced by permission of Friends Reunited

Figure 4.5

Once you click the Add button, your friend is sent a message inviting them to confirm you're friends.

If you want to add several people at once, you can add friends from a screen of search results. Browse to your school, using the steps in the 'Finding your former schoolmates' section. Move the mouse over someone and two icons will appear on the right: an envelope to send a message, and a person with a plus sign to add them as a friend. In Figure 4.3, you can see these icons beside the first name because I'm hovering over the top result. Click the person+ icon to add them as a friend.

Accepting friend requests

When somebody wants to be friends with you, you will receive an email telling you so, just like the notes you might have passed in class all those years ago. Log in to your account, and Friends Reunited will tell you about any outstanding friend requests in the middle of the screen – where you can't miss it.

If you hover over Friends on the navbar, a menu pops up with a Friend Requests option. The number of outstanding requests is shown in brackets here too, so you can see how many requests you have waiting for a decision – waiting for you to accept or reject the friendship.

Select Friend Requests (number) to see who wants to add you to their friends list. Hopefully these should be people you recognise, but you can refresh your memory and find out what they've been up to recently by clicking on their names or pictures to view their profiles. Use the Back button to return to the page you started on.

You can click to accept or ignore the friend request. If you ignore the friend request Friends Reunited stops reminding you about it every time you log in (which just feels awkward), but won't send a huffy message back to the requestee telling them that you really don't like them that much. Thankfully. This is supposed to be about social networking, not anti-social networking.

After you click to accept a friend request, you decide which group of friends this person belongs in: is this an acquaintance, or a friend and family member? The group you choose might not be the same as the group that the requestor put you in when they sent the invitation. They might have put you in the acquaintance group, while you put them in your friends group – or vice versa. You'll never know, because you can't see what group somebody has put you in.

> You may well be slightly confused about this, but it makes more sense when you think of how it might work in the real world. You might consider somebody to be your best friend, but they might think of somebody else as their best friend; it's not a relationship that's always mirrored perfectly.

The screen for adding a friend request to your list looks much the same as the screen used for sending a friend invitation (see Figure 4.5).

When you click Add, the friend request disappears from the main window and the friend is added to your friends list.

To find your friends, having added them to your friends list, hover over Friends on the navbar and then select My Friends. You can click through to view somebody's profile, so you can leave them a comment, buzz, or private mail.

Adding a Newsflash

You can use the Newsflash box on your profile to share the latest developments in your life story, similar to a status update on the Facebook site. You only have 140 characters to play with, though, including spaces and punctuation.

This feature isn't as widely used on Friends Reunited as it is on Facebook (or Twitter), but it's a quick and convenient way to update your profile. Your latest Newsflash is always at the top of your list, so as you add a new one, it pushes the older ones down the list. Your profile visitors can see your ten latest Newsflashes on screen at once, and can click to see older Newsflashes. Newsflashes are all time-stamped, so they can provide a brief snapshot of what you've been doing (or thinking), and when.

When you click on the green-tinted Newsflash box, Friends Reunited helps you out with some sentence starters, as you can see in Figure 4.6.

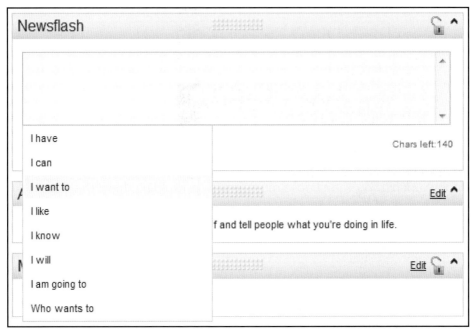

Reproduced by permission of Friends Reunited

Figure 4.6

You can select one of these ice-breakers (overwriting anything already in the text box), or you can start typing. Keep an eye on the countdown underneath the text box on the right, which shows you how many characters you have remaining. If you're still typing but nothing's coming up in the box, you've run out of space.

When you've finished, click the Add Newsflash button. Your Newsflash is saved on your profile with the current date and time.

Why not try adding a Newsflash now, even if only to say that you're experimenting with Friends Reunited? If you make a mistake or if you just change your mind about posting something, you can easily delete it. Just click the X-shaped cross to the right of a Newsflash. Beware though, as there's no confirmation stage and you can't recall a Newsflash you've deleted.

Adding photos and videos

You can enhance your Friends Reunited profile by adding photos and videos and organising them into albums for sharing with other site members. This might sound complicated, but read on for simple instructions (noting of course that you will need to have some digital images stored on your computer to start with).

Choose My Photos under the Profile option on the navbar to start. On the left, you'll find a button to Add Photos.

When you click the link to select the photo files you'd like to upload, a file browser window opens. You can choose multiple files by holding down the Control key on the keyboard, while you click each file once. When you've selected all the files you want and they're highlighted, click the Open button at the bottom right of the window.

You can now choose which album to put your photos in. If they go into the public album, they'll be visible to everyone. If you want to have more control over who sees them, you can choose to create a new album and restrict access to this to people on your friends list.

Click Upload, and then go and make a cup of tea. If these are images from a digital camera, you might have to wait five minutes or so for them to upload. There's an on-screen progress bar to show you how quickly your pictures are uploading, though, so you can tell if you've got time for another Hobnob.

Once they've uploaded, you'll have a chance to add a description of the photos, and details of where and when they were taken.

Tagging photos

As with Facebook, you can label photos with people's names, and this is called *tagging*. Every site member has an album that shows photos in which they're tagged. This means that there is one place you can go to view all the photos your friends have uploaded (and tagged) of you, even though those photos might otherwise exist in dozens of separate albums across Friends Reunited.

To tag a photo, go into your photos, choose the appropriate album, and then click one of the photos so you can view it enlarged. To tag someone, you draw a box around their head. Click in the top left of this box, hold the mouse button down and drag the mouse to the bottom right. When you release your finger from the mouse button, a window pops up asking you who this person is. You can select somebody from your friends list, or you can enter the name if the person isn't yet one of your friends, as shown in Figure 4.7. If the person isn't even on Friends Reunited yet, you can invite them to join.

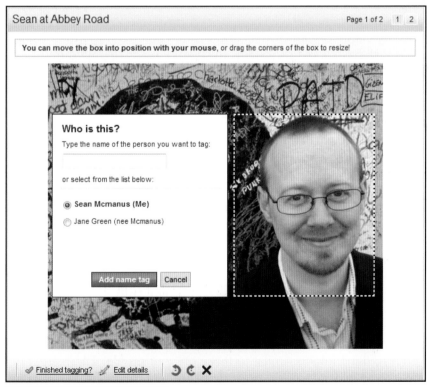

Figure 4.7

If there are several people in a photo, you need to tag them one at a time. The site asks you whether you want to add another tag or whether you've finished now after you've added each tag.

If somebody tags you in error, or tags you in a teenage shot with acne and hair that would scare a bear, you can use the Remove Tag link underneath a photo to dissociate yourself from it.

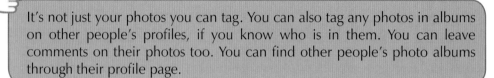

It's not just your photos you can tag. You can also tag any photos in albums on other people's profiles, if you know who is in them. You can leave comments on their photos too. You can find other people's photo albums through their profile page.

Adding videos

With the popularity of camcorders and digital cameras with video capabilities, you might well have some short films to share. Friends Reunited hosts videos of up to 10MB in size, which means you're limited to short snippets, with the length depending on the video quality.

The process for adding videos is the same as for photos, except that you choose My Videos from the navbar instead of My Photos. At the end of uploading, you'll have a delay before your big screen debut, though, because you'll have to wait for the video to be converted.

Friends Reunited say they review every video and reject any that are inappropriate for the privacy settings. If you're worried about whether a particular video will be approved, make sure it goes into a folder that's only accessible to your friends and family so that it doesn't corrupt the general public!

Finding like-minded people in groups

Friends Reunited makes it easy for people with similar interests to discuss them and share photos, using folders similar to those on your profile. There are thousands of groups sorted into categories – including cars, arts and crafts, music, family and relationships, fashion, gardening, films and health. Whatever you're interested in, there's bound to be at least one group to match it, and probably several. There are over 160 groups dedicated to enjoying retirement.

To start looking for a group to join, select Find a Group from the navbar. You'll find it on the menu that appears when you hover over the Groups link on the navbar. You can search for a group by keyword, or browse groups by category. The categories include arts and crafts, cars and motoring, enjoying retirement, computers, books, family, and green issues.

If you click a category, you will see a list of the groups in that category. The groups are sorted by the number of members in descending order. That means the groups higher up the screen are likely to be busier, with more discussion going on.

For each group in a category or search results listing, you can see its name, a short description, the category it's in, and how many members it has. You can join the group immediately using a link that appears on the right when you hover over it, but I wouldn't recommend it. For most interests you'll have a choice of several groups, and for others you should probably drop in first to see whether the group seems to be the right one for you. To take a look at the group without joining, click on the group's name.

Each group has a Group Profile page that looks similar to the one shown in Figure 4.8.

You can join the group from this page at any time, but Friends Reunited is smart enough to join you up automatically if you try to participate in the group, by joining in a discussion, for example. If only all sites were that intuitive.

The Message Boards box shows you recent discussions in the group. As the term 'message board' might suggest, this is an open forum. Any group member can pin their messages to the board, and anybody walking past can read them. Rather than having a random bunch of notes, message boards organise discussions into 'threads'. Each thread concerns one subject. It's like having a piece of string that joins all the related scraps of paper together. So the gardening group I'm browsing has one thread about strawberries, one about tomatoes, and another about rhubarb. You can have more than one thread on a subject, in the same way

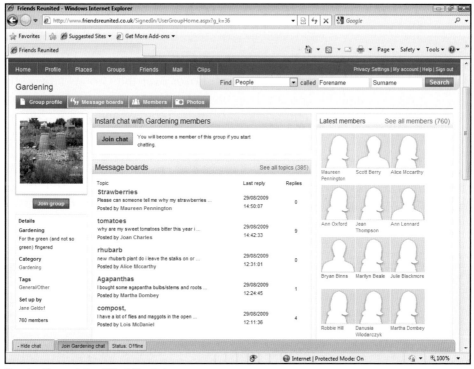

Reproduced by permission of Friends Reunited

Figure 4.8

that you could have similar conversations down the pub on different days or at different tables.

Discussions on a message board can last for weeks, with people chipping in as often as they like and coming back to old threads later.

When you click one of the discussion topics, you see the post that kicked off the discussion, together with all the replies down the screen. The most recent replies are shown towards the top of the screen, so sometimes you'll need to scroll down and read them backwards to understand what was said before.

To reply to a topic, type your response in the second speech bubble down, immediately underneath the original question and beside your profile picture, as shown in Figure 4.9.

Reproduced by permission of Friends Reunited

Figure 4.9

It's annoying for everyone if ten people all post exactly the same response, without paying any attention to each other. If you have similar experience to share, it's okay to reply, but your post will be better received if it acknowledges others who have said the same thing before you. You might say something like: "I had the same results as Dave. The one thing I would add is . . ."

When you click the Reply button, your post is added to the top of the thread. If you go back to the Group Profile page, using the group's own navbar above the horizontal blue line, you'll find the topic you discussed has jumped to the top of the list, because it's the one that's been most recently changed.

To browse more topics, you can click on the Message Boards link to view all topics, and page through them using the Page links at the top of the Topics box.

Starting a topic discussion

Before starting a topic discussion, you should search the past topics to see whether there's an existing discussion you can join. You might even find that your question has been answered before, in which case you can get an immediate reply, and longer-serving members will be spared the same old conversation. The topic search is at the top of the Topics list on the Message Boards page.

You can start a discussion from the Group Profile or the Message Boards pages. You just need to enter your topic subject and your topic message in the Add Topic box, and then click Add.

Your topic needs to sell your thread as being worth reading, even though there are lots of others beside it. Don't use hype, though. Just try to make your subject as specific as possible. A topic like 'my garden' won't mean much in a forum dedicated to gardeners. Even 'big gardens problems' could be better if it were refined to be 'managing large lawns' or 'controlling pests in large gardens'. The more specific your topic subject, the more likely it is to lead to well-informed responses.

You've got plenty of space for your message, but don't feel you have to use it. Brevity is king. To make it as easy as possible for others to grasp your intended topic, keep your message to three sentences, or at most three short paragraphs.

Inviting your friends to join a group

Why not invite others to the group? Click the Invite Friends to Join button on the Group Profile, Message Boards, Photos or Members pages for the group. When you click that button, you'll be shown your friends list. Tick the box underneath any friends you'd like to invite, and Friends Reunited sends them an invitation. Note that you can only invite people who are on your friends list. If you'd like to invite people who aren't on the list, you need to make them friends first, or drop them an email to tell them about the group.

Joining live chats

Chats are one of the best features of Friends Reunited. You can pop into a friendly group and see what others are typing, as they type it. It's a bit like going to a coffee morning (if you make your own coffee).

Each group on Friends Reunited can have one chat discussion running at once, with up to 20 members participating. During a chat, people type in and exchange messages in real time. The messages aren't stored anywhere – they're just like a conversation. They're history when the last person stops talking.

> This isn't like a Facebook chat, where you chat one to one with your contacts. On Friends Reunited, you chat with several people from a group at once, and you can't control who's in the chat room.

You'll see the Chat bar at the bottom of the screen when you're browsing the group pages (see Figure 4.8). You can click Hide Chat to minimise it, but this only tidies up the screen. In Friends Reunited, nobody can see that you're online, and nobody else can invite you to a chat.

To find out what chats are taking place now, go into the Groups section (if you're not already there), and click the Status button on the brown navbar at the bottom of the screen to go online. Click the new button that appears to see Chats Taking Place Now.

You'll see a handful of current chats highlighted in the pop-up menu that opens. You can click the link at the bottom of them to view all chats taking place. When you do that, you can see how many people are already chatting in a group, and when the chat began.

> Just because there's a throbbing green button inviting you to join the chat, it doesn't mean anyone else is there. You might join the chat to find you're all alone. You could still 'join' the chat to see if anyone else joins you, but if you're just looking for a bit of a chin-wag, it's better to start browsing the chats taking place now than it is to start by looking at the groups.

When you join a chat, a chat window will open up in the bottom right corner of the screen, as shown in Figure 4.10. On the right-hand side, you'll see all the people in the chat room. On the left, you'll see what each person says and when they come and go. To start off, why not write 'hello' in the white box on the left. When you click Send or press the Enter key on your keyboard, your words appear in the box above, where everybody can see them. At busy times, there can be a bit of a time lag, but chat rooms come much closer to the immediacy

As the group's founder, you have the honour of kicking off the first discussion. Friends Reunited shows you the Create a Topic form and invites you to start the discussion.

Don't forget to visit your group regularly to contribute to the message board and help it grow. As you make new friend connections, you can invite new people to the group too.

Organising a class reunion

Because Friends Reunited has everybody organised by school and leaving year, it's the ideal tool for organising your class reunion. Using Friends Reunited, you can invite whole years of school leavers and create a reunion message board to manage your plans. You can also email everybody who's expressed an interest without fiddling around with individual emails.

Before organising the reunion, give some thought to the kind of event you'd like to organise. Perhaps you'll have a picnic in the park, with partners and children welcome. Or maybe you'll meet in the pub nearest the school.

Give some thought to the likely numbers, too. If you manage to attract a hundred people, you'll need to book a separate room and will probably need to give six months' notice for that. You'll also need to cover the costs somehow, perhaps by charging for tickets.

It's okay to start with a suggestion, and then see what kind of response it gets.

To start organising your reunion, use the main navbar to go to My Places, find the school you'd like to reunite, and click it. When you're looking at the school's page, which includes former pupils in the middle of it, click the Reunions tab, visible on Figure 4.3 earlier in this chapter.

Once you're in the Reunions section of the site, click Create a Reunion. Friends Reunited asks you first to provide details of the event, including its title, description, venue, and date. You can leave the details to be confirmed later, but the more specific you can be, the easier it is to get people to commit. I picked a date six months ahead and the town of the school, which should be enough for people to work out whether they can be there or not.

If there's a specific anniversary, or other reason for meeting up this year, make sure you include it in your details. Use it to encourage people to meet up now. Who knows when the next reunion will be?

When you click the button to advance to the Next step, you get to pick your invitees and create your invitation, as shown in Figure 4.11.

Create a reunion

1 Details   **2 Invitations**   **3 Finished**

Invite members to your reunion by selecting their leaving years

Years from

| 1980 ▼ |

Years to

| 1984 ▼ |

You are inviting **118 members** who left between 1980 and 1984

To take another look at the School members, open a new window here

You can also personalise your invite   Chars left: 415

Hi there! Hope to see everyone again at this reunion. Let me know if you can make it!

The invite will look like this

Reunion	Class of 1980 Reunion
Description	Has it really been 30 years? Find out what happened to your old classmates by coming to this reunion. If you're in touch with others who aren't on the site, please bring them along, but do let me know...
Hosted by	Sean Mcmanus

Figure 4.11

You can invite people from as many leaving years as you like, but they have to be consecutive. You can invite those who left between 1950 and 1975, for example.

The table shows the different parts of your profile, including your Newsflash, comments, interests, friends, future plans, and Weemee (a cartoon representation of yourself). For each item in the table, you can select whether it can be accessed by:

- **All Friends Reunited members:** Non-members can't view anything, but if they wanted to, they could just register for free. You should think of this group as being the general public; it includes many people you know, but also everybody else who uses the website.

- **Acquaintances, friends and family:** Select this option if you would like to exclude the general public, and would like all your friends list members to have access to it.

- **Friends and family only:** By selecting this option, you restrict access to those who are in the Friends and Family group of your friends list.

To set your privacy levels, choose one radio button on each row of the table. Figure 4.12 shows what mine looked like after I limited my Newsflash to friends and family, and my comments to everybody on both my friends lists.

On the right side, you can see a preview of what your profile will look like to the different groups of people. In Figure 4.12, the comments and Newsflash sections have both disappeared from the preview because you're looking at the profile as seen by the general public, and those sections have been restricted to those on my friends list.

When you're finished, scroll down and click the Save button.

 Your changes may be saved when you click another link, even if you don't click Save. Before leaving this screen, make sure that it reflects the privacy settings you would like to enforce.

Managing friends lists

What happens if you have friends on the wrong list? Perhaps your relationship with someone has changed, so you'd like them to see more (or less) of your profile, or maybe you have decided to carve up your profile differently and want to move people between lists to help you manage your privacy.

After going in to your privacy settings, click on the Friends link on the left. You'll be shown a list of your friends and which list they are on. You can also sever your link with a friend here, and even remove and block them so that their communications to you are automatically screened out.

To move people between friends lists, you just need to click the relevant radio button.

There's no Save button on this screen, so your changes are immediately saved. If you move someone to the wrong list, you should move them back again promptly to avoid any confusion later.

You can access the settings for the 'timeline' and photos and videos using the navbar for this section of the site, on the right-hand side and above the blue horizontal line. Your timeline is part of your profile that enables you to create a graph showing major events in your life. You can customise the settings for each event on your timeline, and each folder of photos and videos, similar to the way each box on your profile can be customised. Under the photo privacy settings, you can also disable tagging so that nobody can link you to a photo. When you've changed your settings, click back to the privacy settings for your profile, and click the Save button on that screen.

Summary

- Friends Reunited is one of the oldest social networking sites and has over half the UK population registered

- The information you provide during registration goes into the public parts of your profile

- Add places (schools you went to, universities, companies you worked at) to make it easier to connect with people you know

- Browse a place's page to see who else went there and click through to their profiles

- On a member's profile, you can add a standard message (a buzz), send a private message, or write a public comment

- When you add a friend, you can decide whether they are on your friends and family, or your acquaintance list. Your privacy settings control how much of your profile each list can see

- Your status update is called a Newsflash

- You can upload albums of photos and videos to share with other members

- Groups enable you to share your passions with other members and to chat with them in real time

- Follow Pam Fitchett's example and use Friends Reunited to create a real-life reunion of your old school friends

Brain training

Let's recap with a quiz. No prizes – it's just for fun. Look out for the tricky ones with multiple answers.

1. Of the social networks in this book, Friends Reunited is . . .

a) The biggest

b) The oldest

c) The smallest

d) The fastest growing

2. If you tell Friends Reunited your marital status, it can be seen by . . .

a) People on your friends list

b) People from your school

c) Anybody who is a site member

d) People on your acquaintances list

3. Who can you chat with using Friends Reunited?

a) People on your friends lists, one to one

b) People who went to your school, one to one

c) Up to 20 of your friends at once

d) People who happen to be in the chat room for a particular interest group when you want to chat

4. A good topic title for an angling discussion forum might be . . .

a) Fish

b) Rods and stuff

c) What's the largest carp you've caught?

d) Rivers

5. If you buzz someone, Friends Reunited will . . .

a) Send them a mild electric shock through their keyboard

b) Leave a message on their profile to say you dropped by

c) Delete their profile for inappropriate behaviour

d) Fly an aircraft uncomfortably low over their house

Answers

Q1 – b   Q2 – c   Q3 – d   Q4 – c

Q5 – b

Using Twitter to tell the world what you're doing

5

Equipment needed: Access to a computer with an Internet connection and web browser (see Chapter 1), plus your own email address.

Skills needed: Ability to use a web browser (see Appendix A); understanding of how to register and create your profile (see Chapter 2).

If you're feeling overloaded with information and bamboozled by everything you can do in the social networks you've explored already, Twitter might come as welcome relief. It has just one function: to enable its members to share concise answers to the question "What are you doing?"

How concise? Well, each entry must be no longer than 140 characters. That might seem like a lot, but it's only the length of this paragraph.

Twitter strictly enforces the limit, so members must focus their attention on the most important thing they want to say, and on the briefest way to express them. (Guess how many edits it took me to make the previous paragraph exactly 140 characters.)

Each entry on the site is called a 'tweet' and encapsulates a single thought or idea. You can view all the tweets from a member on their own page, sorted by the date

Famous as a . . .	Name	Twitter ID
Comedian	Eddie Izzard	eddieizzard
Chef	Jamie Oliver	jamie_oliver
Comedian	Jimmy Carr	jimmycarr
Writer, actor, comedian	John Cleese	johncleese
TV presenter	Jonathan Ross	wossy
Actor, director	Kevin Spacey	kevinspacey
Tour de France winner	Lance Armstrong	lancearmstrong
Politician	Mayor of London	mayoroflondon
TV presenter, actress, entrepreneur	Oprah Winfrey	oprah
Entrepreneur	Richard Branson	richardbranson
Basketball player, rapper	Shaquille O'Neal	the_real_shaq
Writer, actor, TV presenter	Stephen Fry	stephenfry
Politician	The UK Prime Minister	downingstreet
Rugby captain	Will Carling	willcarling
Artist	Yoko Ono	yokoono

To see any of these celebrities' Twitter feeds, just put their Twitter ID from the preceding table into the web address after 'Twitter.com/'. So, for example, to see the UK Prime Minister's feed, you would set your web address to be **www.twitter.com/downingstreet**.

Some of the people on Twitter aren't who they say they are. There are five people on Twitter claiming to be comedian Ricky Gervais at the moment, with 4,285 followers between them. Ricky's own website says that he doesn't have a Twitter feed and that they're all fakes. If you want to follow a celebrity, it's worth checking their official website (if they have one) or another reliable source to make sure it's really them.

Why do people pretend to be celebrities? Sometimes it's to parody the celebrity, and other times it's to hoodwink the public.

There's no harm in following these imposters if you enjoy reading their posts. Just don't go booking any theatre or concert tickets on their say-so, or take offence at what they say. And certainly don't publish their tweets in a national newspaper, as *The Times* and *The Telegraph* did when Michael Jackson died and they thought they had a quote from Foreign Secretary David Miliband lamenting the loss. That quote was taken from a fake Twitter feed.

This fakery is different from when celebrities let their managers or PR people tweet on their behalf. That's usually easy to spot, even if the celebrity doesn't admit it's going on. It tends to result in bland tweets, but at least the news is coming from an official source. You can safely trust and follow officially ghost-written tweets.

To find out whether a feed is authorised, try searching for the celebrity's official website using Google (**www.google.com**) and then see if there's a link back to the Twitter feed. If there is, the feed must be genuine. If not, it doesn't necessarily mean the feed is fake – it might just be that they're slow in adding links to their website.

Twitter has started to address the problem of fake tweets by verifying some big name celebrities themselves, and marking those they've been able to verify. Look in the top right corner of the celebrity's profile for the fluffy cloud with a tick in it. If it's there, it means the profile is genuine. If not, again, it doesn't necessarily mean it's a fake – in most cases it will mean that Twitter hasn't got around to verifying this account yet. Figure 5.2 shows what the verified logo looks like on Kevin Spacey's profile.

This logo means Twitter has checked the account belongs to the celebrity named

Reproduced from Twitter©

Figure 5.2

The independent website Valebrity (**www.valebrity.com**) is also trying to validate celebrity profiles.

I've verified all the Twitter accounts in the previous table. I've left off a few big names using Twitter because it hasn't been possible to verify they're genuine through a credible third-party source. Perhaps you'll come across those as you explore Twitter yourself?

Why not see if your favourite celebrities are on Twitter? For a more extensive directory of celebrities on Twitter, visit **www.celebritytwitter.com** or **www.wefollow.com**.

Creating your Twitter account

Now it's time to try your hand at setting up a Twitter account of your own. Twitter doesn't have friend relationships like Facebook. Instead you can follow someone, which basically means you subscribe to receive all of their tweets. Sometimes the relationship is reciprocal, and people follow you back. But it doesn't have to be that way; it's not a two-way deal, like friend relationships are.

Creating an account on Twitter enables you to do two things: first, you can follow people, so that you can keep up with their tweets, and second, you can share your own ideas and discoveries with the Twitter community.

During registration, Twitter will suggest people you could follow, but you should only add them if you're genuinely interested in them. It's better to follow a few hand-picked people than an army of strangers.

Posting your first tweet

Twitter is different from most social networks, in that the vast majority of the activity takes place in public. As you saw earlier, you didn't even have to register to see my Twitter feed. There is a way to use Twitter to send private messages (see 'Sending private messages on Twitter', later in this chapter) and to restrict your tweets to those you've approved (see 'Managing your privacy and blocking spam', later in this chapter). But Twitter is at its best when everything is out in the open.

Because Twitter is a public forum, you're able to attract readers who are interested in what you have to say, irrespective of who you are or whether they already know you.

To post your first tweet, click on the Home link on the main navbar. Your homepage is also where you read the tweets from those you're following. My example homepage looks like Figure 5.3, although yours won't have any tweets on it if you haven't followed anyone yet.

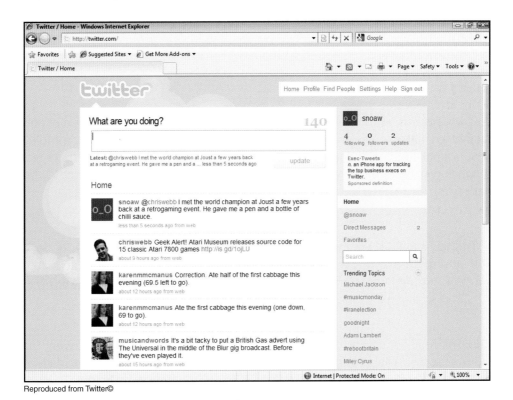

Reproduced from Twitter©

Figure 5.3

At the top of the screen, it asks 'What are you doing?' and gives you a box to reply. Whatever you enter in this box will be your first tweet, and will be available to the general public.

There's no need to be paranoid, but that doesn't mean you should throw all caution to the wind: people often tweet to say they're at the airport with a long flight ahead of them, or they're looking forward to tonight's play. When too much detail is shared, it provides people with intimate knowledge of your comings and goings. And that includes any burglars who might be casing your house. Consider the security implications of anything you post, particularly relating to your whereabouts at any particular time.

Remember, each tweet is restricted to 140 characters. As you type into this box, you'll see the number of remaining characters count down, just above the top right corner of the box. Keep an eye on this number because Twitter won't stop you from typing when you reach your limit. It will just disable the Update button until you cut back. When you get below 10 characters, you'll see the numbers go red as a warning.

I know what you're thinking! You *could* just split your message over two tweets, but that's really not in the spirit of Twitter. Each tweet is supposed to be a complete idea, not half an idea. If you have any idea how to do it, you *could* use text speak to cut down the number of characters ('use txtspk 2 ct dwn no of chrctrs'), but that's tiring for readers to decode.

The art of Twitter is to focus on the most important thing you want to say, and then find the shortest way to say it. You might find it helps to speak aloud as you're writing – anything that sounds unnatural in speech can probably be edited so that it's shorter.

It doesn't really matter what you enter for your first tweet. You could tweet that you're 'reading a fabulous book: Social Networking for the Older and Wiser', 'listening to the Bee Gees on the radio', or 'experimenting with Twitter'.

When you click on the Update button, your tweet appears on both your homepage and your profile.

Shortening website addresses

People often use Twitter to share articles, videos, games, or other content they've found on the Internet. To make life easier, any website addresses in your tweet will be turned into links automatically.

The drawback is that sometimes the website address can consume a large chunk of your allocated characters, leaving you no room to explain what you're sharing, or why you're sharing it!

If you wanted to direct people to the Welsh village with the longest name in Britain, for example, you'd only have 64 characters left to talk about it, after you'd entered the name of the domain: **http://www.llanfairpwllgwyngyllgogerychwyrndrobwllllantysiliogogogoch.co.uk**.

There are services that you can use to shorten a website address. They work like this: you enter the website address you'd like shortened, and they give you a new, shorter address to put in your tweet. When people click the link in your tweet, very cleverly, they're redirected to your link.

One such service is at **http://bit.ly**. When I entered my Welsh village address (I'm not repeating it here!), it was shortened from 75 characters to 20.

At its simplest, all you need to do on the bit.ly homepage is enter your website address and click on the Shorten button. Refer to Figure 5.4.

This provides you with a shorter website address (URL) you can copy and paste. I can now put **http://bit.ly/12JrJR** into my tweet to direct people to the village's website.

Okay, so the example above is a bit silly, but a link to a BBC news story can be about 50 characters, which is over a third of the space available for a tweet.

There's much more you can do at bit.ly, including tweeting directly from that site, but I recommend you stick with using Twitter to avoid overcomplicating things.

Many similar services are available, including at **www.tinyurl.com** and **www.is.gd**.

Reproduced from Bit.ly™

Figure 5.4

Because you can't see where a link is leading, take care with clicking on links. People will sometimes post links with enticing descriptions to try to persuade people to visit dodgy websites. Review other tweets from the same person to see what kind of reputation they deserve before clicking on anything you're unsure about. This isn't a big problem, but it doesn't hurt to be cautious.

Finding people to follow on Twitter

Now you have a Twitter account, you can follow anybody on Twitter so that when you log in you'll see their latest tweets on your homepage. To follow people you just click on the Follow button underneath their photo when you're looking at their Twitter profile. If you can't see a Follow button, it's probably because you need to log in first.

If you want, you can start by following Jonathan Ross or Stephen Fry. (Note that Twitter is the only place you can do this without getting arrested!) Just visit their Twitter profiles and click on the Follow button underneath their photographs. If you want to follow me, you can go to **www.twitter.com/musicandwords** and click on my Follow button.

If you want to see Twitter's suggestions for people you could follow, click on Find People in the main navbar, and then click Suggested Users. These introductions are randomly selected from a pool of users that Twitter believes represent a good introduction to the site. Tick the box beside any you'd like to follow, and click the large Follow button at the bottom.

Searching for people you already know on Twitter

To start looking for people you know on Twitter, click on the Find People link in the main navbar. You'll see a Search box, which you can use to conduct a name search.

The search results are sorted so that those who have the most followers are nearest the top of the screen. You might have to scroll and page through the results (clicking the Next button at the foot of each page) to find the person you're looking for. You can use the Follow button on the search results page to start following someone, or you can click through to their profile to see what they've tweeted lately and use the Follow button there.

This Search box is only supposed to be used to search for people by name, so it's not ideal for finding people according to their interests. But many people do embed their interests in their username, so it's worth trying the odd keyword here to see what it throws up (e.g. angling, music, dogs).

Finding people who tweet about your interests

There's no easy way to search the biographies that people add to their Twitter profiles, but you can find like-minded people with a bit of detective work. If you search for individual tweets on a topic that interests you, you can trace them back to their authors. Elementary, my dear reader.

To search tweets, go to your homepage (using the Home link on the main navbar), and then enter keywords in the Search box on the right-hand side, as shown in Figure 5.3. When you click on the magnifying glass, or press the Enter key on the keyboard, Twitter searches all the public tweets for your keywords. You'll see the most recent at the top of the screen, with the rest sorted in time order, going backwards. If you see someone or something that intrigues you, click the author's profile picture. Their profile opens, and from there you can review all their tweets (to see if they're consistently worth reading), and can click the Follow button to subscribe to their tweets.

Sometimes you'll see users have created lists of people they follow, shown in the margin of their profile. If you find a relevant themed list, you can follow everybody on it with a single click, or pick and choose who to follow.

At www.wefollow.com, there's a directory of Twitter users, sorted by interest. It's worth browsing there to see who you can find.

Should you follow people back?

You'll be sent an email when somebody follows you, including a link to check out their profile. You can then choose to follow them back, if you're interested in what they're writing, but you don't have to do this. That's one of the reasons the platform's been popular with celebrities; they can have millions of followers, even though they only really want to follow twenty people themselves.

Try not to feel honour-bound to follow people just because they're following you. If you do that, you'll soon find your homepage is clogged with tweets that you don't really want to see.

Don't ask people to follow you, even if you're following them. It just comes across as a bit desperate. If you want somebody to consider following you, send them an interesting message. They'll probably check out your profile, and if they like what they see, they'll choose to follow you then.

Reading the tweets from those you're following

Whenever you log in, you'll be taken to your homepage, as in Figure 5.3. This shows the latest tweets from everybody you're following, sorted by time with the latest at the top. Your own tweets also appear here, so you can follow the whole conversation if you've been replying in public to any of these tweets.

If you want to find one person you're following and read just their tweets, you can either click on their username or profile photo next to one of their tweets, or you can browse everyone you're following by clicking the 'following' number on the right-hand side.

If you see something you might want to find again later, such as a link or interesting photo, you can mark it as one of your 'favorites'. Hover over the tweet and you'll see a star icon appear on the right-hand side. If you click that, the tweet will be added to your favorites and can be found again by clicking on the Favorites link on the right-hand side of your homepage. Favorites appear on your profile, so don't mark anything as a favorite unless you're happy for your association with that tweet to be public.

Sending replies and messages to people on Twitter

If you want to send another Twitter member a message, you can either do it in public or in private. If your message, or the expected reply, is likely to be of interest to others and could spark a conversation, then send it in public. If you're asking something that's only relevant to the two of you (such as what time you're meeting up later), then it's best sent in private. That said, the beauty of Twitter is that it provides insight into people's everyday lives, so feel free to tweet about what you're having for dinner and what you're watching on TV – the kinds of things that wouldn't normally justify an email, but which are the texture of our daily lives.

To send a public message, you just tweet the @ symbol, the addressee's username, and then the message you'd like to send. There's no space between the @ sign and the username and you still only have 140 characters, including the addressee's username. Here's an example tweet addressed to musicandwords:

@musicandwords which is the best London museum?

When you send this message, it will be seen by the addressee and all of your shared followers. Anyone can read it if they come across your profile page, where all your tweets are published.

When the addressee replies, he or she will use your username with an @ sign before it, to make sure the reply gets to you. To see your @ messages, click where it says @yourusername on the right side of your homepage.

It's rude to talk about people behind their backs, so the @ sign is also used when you're talking *about* people, so they can 'hear' you by checking their @ messages. Look at the example below for a clearer idea on this.

You might tweet something like:

Going to see the cinema later with @musicandwords

If you see a tweet you want to reply to, hover your mouse over it, and you'll see a curved arrow appear on the right-hand side of it. If you click that to reply, the sender's username and the @ sign will be put into your tweet automatically. You can reply to any message (even if it wasn't addressed to you), and can reply to several people at once by including all their usernames and putting an @ sign before each one.

Bear in mind that tweets aren't shown in context in the timeline; it's not like an email, where you can see what's being replied to in the same message as the reply. Each tweet is an independent statement, so make sure your meaning will be clear, and that it's obvious which tweet you're replying to if you don't say so.

Any username preceded by an @ sign is turned into a link to that person's profile, including all their tweets. So if you're mystified as to why somebody is tweeting "@username three badgers and a trifle", you can click the link to ferret out the person and/or tweet that might have prompted that reply!

Tweets that are sent using the reply arrow also have a link underneath them on the timeline. If you click on In Reply To [name] underneath a tweet, it'll show you the tweet that prompted the reply. Don't count on people doing that, though.

You can send @ messages to anyone using Twitter, irrespective of whether you follow each other. That means you can use Twitter to send messages to celebrity users. Be warned, though, that it looks a bit sad if you only ever send messages to famous people. It's like hanging around the back of the stage door all day, hugging an autograph book.

Sending private messages on Twitter

You can also send private messages to your followers. These are known as 'direct messages' and are only seen by the addressee. By default, users receive an email to tell them when they've received a direct message, although they can turn that off.

To send a direct message, you use the letter 'd', followed by a space and the username you'd like to address. You then write the rest of the message. Again, you've got just 140 characters to play with and you can address only one person at a time. Figure 5.5 shows an example direct message.

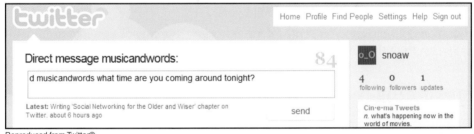

Reproduced from Twitter©

Figure 5.5

If you've done it right, you'll see that above your tweet box, it recognises that you're writing a direct message and who you're addressing it to.

Don't worry if that all seems a bit complex. There is an easier but slower way. If you go to someone's profile, there's a pull-down menu at the top of it that opens when you click the star. From there, you can send a direct message or mention someone in a tweet.

Summary of messaging on Twitter

The differences between the different message types on Twitter can be confusing, but this table summarises the key differences:

Direct messages versus replies on Twitter

	Direct message	Reply
How do you address it?	d username	@username
Can the addressee see it?	Yes	Yes
Do your followers see it?	No	Yes, if they also follow the addressee
Do the addressee's followers see it?	No	Yes, if they also follow you
Does it appear on your public profile page where anyone can find it?	No	Yes
Who can you send it to?	Only your followers	Anybody on Twitter
How many people can you send a message to at the same time?	One	As many as you can fit into 140 characters with your message

Forwarding messages with 're-tweeting'

If somebody tweets something you'd like to share with your followers, you're free to 'retweet' it, which is a bit like forwarding an email. It's one of the ways that ideas spread quickly through the Twitter community.

When you hover over a tweet on your homepage, a link appears on the right to retweet it. When you do so, it is added to your profile and to your followers' homepages, with a recycling symbol beside it (see the third tweet in Figure 5.1).

This is a relatively new feature. Before it was introduced, the Twitter community created its own convention, and you might still come across this. It worked by cutting and pasting the tweet into a new tweet, and adding information on where it had come from. Users wrote RT (for retweet) at the start, followed by an @ sign, the originator's name, and the tweet content. Here's an example retweet using that convention:

> RT @musicandwords: How do frogs die? They kermit suicide.

Thankfully, that level of complexity is quickly becoming a thing of the past – so don't worry about it.

Joining the conversation with hashtags

Because each tweet is independent, it can be difficult to have a proper conversation and keep track of it. Hashtags are used to organise tweets into groups, so that it's possible for people to find tweets about the same subject. They're most often used for topics that affect everybody or have widespread appeal, such as for sharing reactions to current news headlines, or jokes and puns.

A hashtag is a short code word, preceded by the hash character (#). If you see one in a tweet, you can click it to see all the other tweets that include that hashtag. If you want to reply, you can just copy the hashtag to the end of your tweet.

For example, if you see the tweet:

> Not sure which way to vote on Wednesday #UKelection

You could click on the hashtag (#UKelection) at the end to view other people's views on the election. If you wanted to add your own view, you'd just need to put the same hashtag (#UKelection) at the end.

You can make up your own hashtags too, to make it easy for people to find tweets on the same subject – although if it's something that's only likely to appeal to your followers, it's unlikely to be worthwhile.

To view all the tweets featuring a particular hashtag, you can just type that hashtag into the Search box on the right-hand side of your Twitter homepage. If you enter it without the hash sign, you might also discover some other relevant tweets that used the keyword in their content rather than as a hashtag.

Popular hashtags include #followfriday, where people recommend other Twitter users for people to follow on a Friday, and #musicmonday, where people start the week by recommending a band to their followers.

Be careful about entering your password into websites or applications that don't belong to Twitter. Many of them are trustworthy, but some could be used to hijack your account to send unwanted emails (spam). Make sure that you can find an endorsement from a reliable source before trusting a third-party application. (It doesn't count if it's on the application's own website!) In particular, I'd steer clear of any site that offers you money for tweeting, or guarantees to find you hundreds of followers.

Managing your privacy and blocking spam

Just as soon as somebody invents a new communication channel, someone else creates a way to abuse it for unscrupulous marketing purposes. From the doorbell to the email, junk messages follow us everywhere. Spam (in the form of unwanted advertising) is a problem on Twitter, as it is on email, but it takes a slightly different form.

On Twitter, 'spammers' register an account and then follow you. When you click to look at their profile, you see their advert, usually in the biography or in tweets that repeat the same link. Because the spammer is following you, anyone viewing your Twitter profile can then click through to see the spam profile too.

There is a way to stop your account becoming associated with spammers. On the right-hand side of every Twitter profile is a link to report the member as a spammer. If you click it, they will be stopped from following you and Twitter will investigate the account to see if it should be banned.

You can also block any other member, which stops them from following you. Be aware, though, that this won't stop them from being able to read what you write on Twitter. As you saw at the start of the chapter, you don't even have to register to read most of the content on Twitter.

If you want to restrict your tweets to those you've explicitly authorised, you can 'protect' your tweets. This means that new followers need to seek your permission to follow you and read your tweets. To protect your tweets, carry out the following steps: click on Settings in the main navbar and scroll down to the bottom. Tick the box to protect your tweets and click to save. Simple. Your tweets are now protected, although some old tweets might still be available in some places.

New followers who want to see your Twitter feed see only your biography, and a message that says your tweets are protected and they need to send a request to follow you.

If they do send a request, you'll receive an email telling you about it. Your options are to accept the request, decline the request, or block the sender so that they cannot send any further requests.

When you protect your updates, your existing followers remain on your account, but you can click the Followers link on your profile to block any that you want to lose as followers. Just click on Actions to the right of the person you'd like to block, and then select Block, as shown in Figure 5.7.

Reproduced from Twitter©

Figure 5.7

Protecting your tweets stops you from getting the greatest benefit from Twitter. It dramatically cuts the number of followers you have, because people can't see what you're tweeting before deciding to send a follow request.

Part of the appeal of Twitter is that everyone can join in. By restricting who can see your tweets, you limit the potential of your ideas to reach new people.

Unless you're on the run, or have another good reason to keep your tweets secret, you should leave your tweets unprotected.

Summary

- Content on Twitter is usually public, although you can protect your tweets

- You can follow famous people on Twitter, but should check they're genuine

- A post on Twitter (a tweet) is limited to 140 characters

- You can use sites like bit.ly to shorten website addresses so they fit more easily into a tweet

- If someone follows you, you do not have to follow them back

- Use @username to send a public message

- Use d username, or the Direct Message link on someone's profile, to send a private message

- To share others' tweets with your followers, 'retweet' them

- Use hashtags to provide context to your tweets

- You can share pictures using Twitpic

- Report spammers and block anyone you don't want following you

Brain training

Here's a quick quiz to help you review some of the key points in this chapter. As usual, there might be multiple right answers for a question.

1. A tweet is . . .

a) A toy for a budgie

b) Someone who uses Twitter

c) A message of up to 140 characters shared on Twitter

d) A link on Twitter

2. By default, who can see your tweets?

a) Only people who follow you

b) Only members of Twitter

c) Anyone

d) Only the people you follow

3. Who sees a message you address to another user with @?

a) The addressee

b) The addressee's followers

c) Your followers

d) Your shared followers

e) Anybody who sees your public profile

4. Who can read a direct message?

a) The addressee

b) The addressee's followers

c) Your followers

d) Anybody who sees your profile

5. If your message won't fit, it's a good idea to . . .

a) Shorten the links

b) Use shorter words

c) Split it over several tweets

d) Use text speak

Answers

Q1 – c   **Q2** – c   **Q3** – a, d and e   **Q4** – a

Q5 – a and b

PART III
Joining specialist communities and starting your own

It's a shame about your mother getting eaten by a shark. On the other hand, our holiday photo album looks awesome!

Connecting with other seniors at Saga Zone

Equipment needed: Access to a computer with an Internet connection and web browser (see Chapter 1), plus your own email address.

Skills needed: Ability to use a web browser (see Appendix A); understanding of how to register and create your profile (see Chapter 2). Over 50 years of life experience (not because it's difficult, but because there's an age barrier!).

The social networks explored so far in this book have been open to all comers, with groups forming within them to cater for different hobbies, interests, and age groups. If you have followed the instructions in Chapters 3 to 5 regarding logging onto Facebook, Friends Reunited, and Twitter, registering and completing your online profile, you should now be feeling quite experienced in these areas. The processes are very similar for the networks described in this third part of the book: Saga Zone, Eons, Meetup, and Ning.

In this chapter, you'll explore Saga Zone (**www.sagazone.co.uk**), which is exclusively for the 50-plus age group. This social network has been created by the Saga Group, which is based in the UK and provides services including insurance and holidays for the over 50s.

At Saga Zone, you can network with 55,950 other seniors in forums and clubs. Saga Zone also makes it easy to create a blog, and organise real-world social gatherings. Saga Group itself has organised overnight cruises for members to meet other Saga Zoners face to face, with a programme of entertainment and educational activities on board.

Although registration is quick and easy, you might encounter problems if someone else in your house has already registered. Saga Zone's terms and conditions, in common with many other social networks, say that you can only have one account per person. If Saga Zone detects multiple accounts at the same PC, it lets you know and provides contact details so you can ask the techies to enable your account. The rule is in place to protect the community from people who might abuse the site.

Saga Zone uses nicknames to refer to members on the site. The other information you provide during registration is kept private, but your profile and any content posted is public.

At the end of the registration process, Saga Zone confirms your email address and password onscreen, so it can be read on your monitor. Don't sign up in a public place (where your password might be seen by passers-by) and don't put anything rude in your password if there are kids looking over your shoulder!

Finding your bearings on Saga Zone

Follow the usual procedure (see Chapter 2) to register at Saga Zone. After registering, you arrive at the news page, where you can read about the latest developments on the site. It looks like Figure 6.1.

The large blue buttons at the top of the screen take you to:

● The *news*, with all the news about the site. This is the home page of the site.

● *Friends*, showing all your friends on the site.

● The *forums*, where people are discussing everything from oven cleaning to philosophy, and from a charity mountain climb to flatulence.

● *Messages*, where you can write messages to other site members or read their replies.

● The *gallery* of the latest photos.

Figure 6.1

- The *blogs*, where you can read what people have been posting in their public journals.

- The *clubs*, where people can share their interests through photos, videos, and chats.

- The *calendar*, where you can see the events that members are organising.

Above those blue buttons, a white navbar provides links to My Zone, About Me, Things To Do, Search, Help, Contact Us, and House Rules. You sometimes need to use these links to access features, such as editing your account details, or to seek help with using the site. Most of the functions in these links are repeated in the blue buttons below, though. Where you have a choice, try using the blue buttons first – for one thing, they're much easier to find. On some pages the blue buttons disappear. You can bring them back by clicking on the My Zone link.

To edit your profile, hover over About Me and then click Edit My Profile in the pop-up menu that appears.

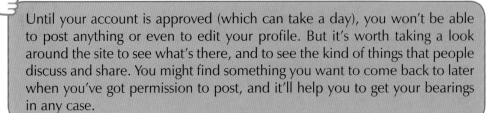

Until your account is approved (which can take a day), you won't be able to post anything or even to edit your profile. But it's worth taking a look around the site to see what's there, and to see the kind of things that people discuss and share. You might find something you want to come back to later when you've got permission to post, and it'll help you to get your bearings in any case.

Having fun in the forums

The Saga Zone forums are where you go to chat about anything that is of interest to you. The forums are open to all members and have a real sense of fun about them. In the Just For Laughs forum, members can share jokes and engage in word games. There's one discussion where you're asked to post a line from a song that includes one word from the previous lyric posted. There's another where players must think of a person's name that starts with the last letter of the one before. Some of these games have been running for over a year and attracted over 50,000 responses. If you can think of a different forum game, you're welcome to start it.

The forums aren't purely for fun and games, though. There are also places to chat, debate the news, and discuss relationships, health, money, travel, gardening, technology, the working world, and more. At Saga Zone, the forums are the real engine of the site: many members drop in mainly to have a natter on them.

Even if you haven't used a forum before, you'll find it easy to get the hang of them here. Each forum is dedicated to one subject, such as gardening or technology. Inside that forum, there are a number of topics being discussed, such as growing peppers and buying a new PC. Conversations start when somebody opens a topic, suggesting what should be discussed. After that, anybody can add their comments, including multiple times if they want to respond to what others say. Each contribution is known as a post. The whole conversation is organised in time order, from the first post through to the last, and this is known as a 'thread'. Threads are a common feature of social networking sites, and you will come across them frequently.

One thing to beware of is that whatever you post in a forum will be available to every Saga Zone member, and in most cases will also be available to members of the public who aren't registered. Some of the forums are restricted to members only, including the caring forum, social events, new members, and today's birthdays. Check the House Rules for the latest list of member-only forums, and assume everything else is available to everyone.

Browsing forums

To start browsing the forums, click the blue Forums button. You'll be shown a list of forums, together with quick links to the Main Forum Index and the Forum Map on the right-hand side.

I recommend you click New Members to enter a forum that's dedicated to helping you get started. The forum looks like Figure 6.2.

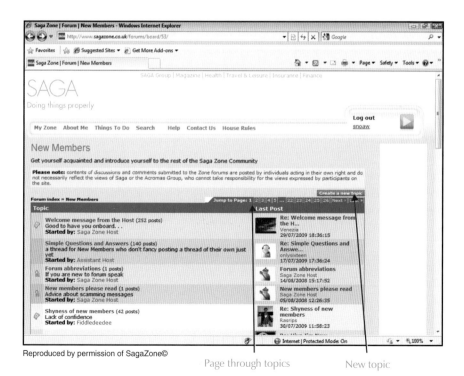

Reproduced by permission of SagaZone©

Page through topics   New topic

Figure 6.2

On the left, you see the discussions. For each one, you can see the discussion topic, which is in bold blue text, how many posts the topic has received, and who started the topic. For many of them you can also see a short description of the topic underneath the topic name.

On the right-hand side, you see the details of the latest post in that topic, including the time and date, and who made the post. This is what's used to sort these topics: those with the most recent contributions are at the top. The topics that are tinted blue are the exception to this sorting rule. To make sure important topics are always easy to find, Saga Zone's hosts have designated them as 'sticky', which means they'll always stick to the top of the list, even if nobody posts anything new to them.

To get to older posts, click the Jump to Page link on the right-hand side at the top of the topic list. You can also click the Prev (short for previous) and Next links to move through the pages. There's a link that takes you straight to the Last page too, although that's not too useful in this context because it takes you to conversations that ended years ago. Any conversation can be reopened just by replying to it, bringing it back to the front page. But for the best results, I recommend you stick to the first few pages, because you can be confident the people in those conversations are still watching and replying.

To view a topic, click its name. The post that started the thread appears at the top. Underneath, the replies start with the oldest and become more recent as you work your way down the screen.

In Figure 6.3, I've scrolled the navbars off the top of the screen, so you can see more of the posts. This post was created by one of Saga Zone's hosts to welcome newcomers. If you're wondering what the 'O word' is, it's 'Oldie'!

I clicked through to page 3 in Figure 6.3, using the links in the blue stripe at the top of the posts. The original post is always onscreen at the top, so you can refer back to what the conversation's supposed to be about, but on page 1 it's also the first post, so you'll see it twice, which can be confusing.

Forums can have more specialist forums inside them – so that, for example, the social events forum includes a separate section dedicated to each geographic

Reproduced by permission of SagaZone©

Figure 6.3

region. When you're looking at a forum's topic list, any sub-forums are listed in a separate box at the top of the screen.

The Forum Map gives you a single-screen overview of all the forums there are, so you don't have to dip into the different categories to find them. From this map, you can go straight into any of the forums. You can go straight to the Forum Map through the Things To Do menu on your navbar, and can also find it by clicking the big blue Forums button.

Don't be afraid to explore the forums. They cover a wide range of different interests, and there's bound to be something there for you. It's okay to just read posts for a while without replying (sometimes called 'lurking'). It helps you to familiarise yourself with the tone and content of the forums.

Navigating the forums with the 'breadcrumb trail'

You may well have no idea what a 'breadcrumb trail' is, but don't be alarmed – it just provides an easy method to find your way around a site and you will soon get the hang of it. At the top of each forum screen, there is a line that looks a bit like this:

Forum index » Social Events » London » Veggies in the Greenwich Area

You remember how Hansel and Gretel left a trail of breadcrumbs so they could find their way home again? Actually, it didn't work for them because the animals ate them all, but never mind. That hasn't stopped the web community from naming this useful navigational tool 'the breadcrumb trail'.

From left to right, the breadcrumb trail shows the main path through the site to reach the current post. In this example, from the Forum index you would go to Social Events, then London, where you would find the Veggies in the Greenwich Area discussion. The trail gives you an idea of how your discussion fits in with the rest of the site, and also provides some context to the discussion. You know the discussion is about a social event in London, for example, which might not be clear from the discussion's title.

The breadcrumb trail is most useful because the phrases between the chevrons are links. If you imagine each section is inside the section to its left in the trail, it gives you an easy way to go up a level and see what else is there. It's a bit like having folders inside folders in Windows. Click London to find all the other discussions about London social events. Click Social Events and you can find out what's happening everywhere, both in and out of London. Click the Forum index to go to the top and explore all the topics, including social events.

Posting to the forums

If you'd like to chip in on a discussion, click the Reply to Topic button underneath the original post, or click the Reply button on any post in the thread. It doesn't matter what you click; your reply goes to the end of the thread in any case.

If you don't see any reply links, check that you're logged in properly. Some of the forums are available to the general public, so you won't be stopped from reading them if you're not signed in; you'll just not be able to write anything.

If you are logged in, it might be that the topic has been locked. The site hosts sometimes lock topics to stop people replying to them. This is usually restricted to official announcements from Saga Zone, and to social events that have already taken place. When you're looking at the topic list, a padlock next to topics indicates that they have been locked.

The form to reply to the topic has a large box for you to type into, with some formatting controls underneath. Most of these controls work by adding special codes into your reply, which can be a bit confusing, so I suggest you stick with plain text and let your carefully chosen words provide emphasis.

There's a Web Link button you can use to add a link, which will prompt you to enter the web page's address and a description for the link. You might find that Internet Explorer mollycoddles you and stops the website from opening up a window for this, in which case you need to click the yellow bar at the top of the screen. It's safe to click the yellow bar and then select Temporarily Allow Scripted Windows. After you've done so, you need to click the Web Link button again to start entering your link.

The Image button enables you to insert only images which are already on the Internet, rather than enabling you to upload images to Saga Zone for sharing. You need to have a link to the image, which you can find by right-clicking a picture on a web page, selecting Properties, and then copying the URL from the box that opens up. That's a lot of work for something so simple though, so I recommend you ignore the Image button here. The best way to share your own photos is to upload them in clubs, which you'll explore shortly.

Quoting somebody else's post

Because the replies always go to the end of the thread, it can be difficult to work out what's being replied to. What if you wanted to pick up a point that somebody raised several posts ago? How would others know what you were talking about? One way is to address the poster (the person who made the post you want to reply to) by name before going into their comment, but that still requires everybody else to scroll up to see what he or she said. A better approach is to quote the post you're replying to. Saga Zone makes this simple.

Beside each post, there's a button that says Quote. If you click the button, you'll be taken to the form to reply to the topic, but you'll see some formatting codes and the post you're replying to already in the box. It might look a bit like this:

[quote name="gilliand" time="30/07/2009 @ 15:15:07"] What else would you spend 46p on?[/quote]

Just click at the end of the last line, and press the Return key twice on your keyboard. You can then type your reply without worrying about getting tangled up in the quoted post. When your reply is submitted the site will unscramble the code and put the quoted post at the top of yours, neatly boxed off. It looks like Figure 6.4.

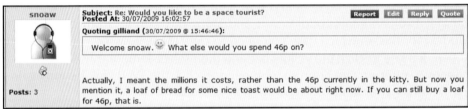

Reproduced by permission of SagaZone©

Figure 6.4

When you post on a topic, or if you click the Subscribe to Topic button at the top or bottom of a topic's posts, you'll be able to keep up with future posts easily. Under the My Zone link on the white navbar, there's a link to My Responses. Check in there regularly to see if anyone's replied to your posts. It enables you to ensure you don't miss out the discussion without having to spend time dipping in and out of the same topics to check for updates.

Starting your own topic

You can easily start your own topic, as a way to kick off a new debate, seek advice, or share something with other community members.

Before you do this, I recommend that you search the forum to see whether a similar discussion is already taking place. It's easier to join an existing conversation than it is to kick one off, and you'll benefit from the input of everyone who's already posted and is subscribed to that thread.

When you hover over Search on the white navbar above the blue buttons, you can select Search Forums from the pop-up menu. You can search by keyword or by poster if you want to see what else somebody's been saying.

If there isn't already a relevant thread, your next step is to find the right forum for it. If you put your message in the wrong place, you won't find the right audience, and so won't get the number or quality of responses you want.

The best way to choose a suitable forum is to go through the Forum Map, which you can find under the Things To Do option on the white navbar. It includes links to take you straight to the forum you need.

Once you arrive in the forum, above the list of existing topics, on the right-hand side, you'll see a Create a New Topic button. It's only small, so if you need a hand finding it, refer back to Figure 6.2.

To create a new topic, you need to provide the:

- **Subject:** This should succinctly describe what your topic is about. Be as specific as possible to ensure that people know what to expect in your thread. The subject is what sells the discussion to potential participants.

- **Description:** This is an optional short statement to provide a bit more detail. It appears in the topic list, so use it to entice people to your discussion. Limit yourself to a sentence or a few words.

- **Message:** This is the meat of the post! I recommend you keep posts to under three medium-sized paragraphs so that people can comfortably read them, but you can write more if you need to. To stimulate discussion, why not finish your post with a question? Just like that.

As with replies, you can use the Preview button to see how the post will look before you click the button to Create a New Topic.

One additional option you have as a topic creator, as opposed to a thread participant, is to create a poll. The pie chart icon on the right of the formatting bar rolls down a box where you can enter a title for the poll and up to five multiple choice answers. Polling is a simple technique to discover other members' views on the topic you have created, and to encourage discussion.

When you create a topic, you're automatically subscribed to it, so you can check for replies by choosing My Responses, under My Zone on the white navbar.

Joining in clubs

As well as forums, Saga Zone provides clubs where people can share their interests. These have additional features, including the ability to post photos and videos. Unlike forums, clubs cannot be accessed by non-members of Saga Zone.

According to Saga, there are 11 million over-50s who are retired in the UK and 65% of them have taken up new hobbies since leaving work. 13% spend five hours or more on their hobby a week. Gardening is the most popular activity (41%), followed by cooking and baking (27%), and photography (25%). 40% complete Sudoku or crossword puzzles. 20% do voluntary work, and 7% have learned a new language.

To find a club, click the blue Clubs button, and you'll be introduced to recently opened clubs. If you click the Browse Clubs link on the right-hand side, you can page through all the clubs. This is a good way to see the breadth of clubs on offer, but the best way to find something you're interested in is to use the Search box at the top of the Browse Clubs screen.

You can enter any of the clubs by clicking its name. When you do so, you'll be automatically joined to that club. The exception to this is if the club has restricted membership. Some of the clubs require application and approval from the club operator, in which case you'll be prompted to enter a message to request membership.

Don't be afraid to pop into clubs to see what's there. You do automatically become a member but if you don't like what you see, you can use the button in the club to resign from the club again.

Once you've joined a club, you can quickly go back there by clicking the blue Clubs button, and then clicking My Clubs, on the right. The start page is called the Club House and looks like Figure 6.5.

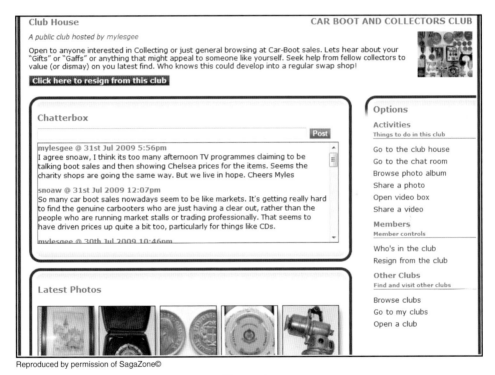

Reproduced by permission of SagaZone©

Figure 6.5

The Chatterbox gives you a quick and simple way to post something; you can just type it and then press the Post button. The box underneath shows you recent chat posts. If you want to add formatting, or see older posts, click the link on the right-hand side to go into the chat room. Take care here because you can't edit or delete what you post, although other members will I'm sure be understanding of any slips.

Further down the screen, you'll see the photos that have been added to the group. If you want to add a photo yourself, click the Share a Photo link on the right-hand side. You'll be asked to browse for its location on your computer, and will then be able to add a title and description using the same formatting editor as you've seen in the forums.

You can only share videos which are already on the video-sharing site YouTube (**www.youtube.com**). If you wanted to add a video in Saga Zone, you'd need to upload it there first, but this feature is usually used to share links to other interesting or entertaining videos you've found on that site.

If you can't find a club for your interests (and there are lots to choose from!), then why not start your own? When you're in the clubs pages, you'll see a link on the right-hand side to Open a Club (refer to Figure 6.5). This only takes a few minutes: you just need to provide a name, description, and picture that represents your club. You can choose to have clubs open to everyone, open to approved members with applications welcome, or only available to invitees.

Once you've created the club, you'll find its administration controls on the right-hand side. If your club is invitation-only, you can then invite other Saga Zone members, even if they're not on your friends list. If your club has restricted access, you can manage applications. You can also send a group email to members.

In the unlikely event you need to police conduct in your club, you can go through the members list (Who's in the Club) and issue a warning or a ban to a member. Saga Zone also keeps an eye on clubs from time to time to make sure the house rules are being followed. Private and application-only clubs enjoy greater freedom than public clubs, so if your topic might come close to breaching the rules, restrict your membership.

Creating a blog

A blog is an easy way to publish content on the Internet. Each entry is time and date-stamped, so blogs are often used like public diaries, with their authors sharing an account of what they've been up to and what they've been thinking about. Blogs can also be used to share creative work, such as poetry. Readers can leave their feedback and comments on what you've written. In some ways, it's like a discussion thread, but whereas discussions are democratic and everyone has an equal say, on a blog you're the boss. Others can leave their comments on what you've written, but it's your publishing platform and only you can make an original post.

To get started, click the blue Blogs button. You'll be shown a selection of recommended blog posts, so pick any of these for a preview of what you'll be creating shortly. The blog post appears at the top, with any comments below that. If you'd like to add your own comment, just click on the Post a Comment link at the end of the post or the Reply link beside any of the existing comments. Unlike forum posts, where all replies go to the end of the list, you can reply to existing comments and have your entry appear underneath what you're replying to, even if that means inserting it half-way down the comments list.

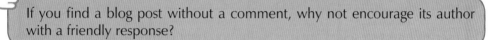

If you find a blog post without a comment, why not encourage its author with a friendly response?

If you'd like to see more blog posts by the same author, click their profile picture and then select Blogs from the right-hand side of their profile page. Unless you have a giant monitor, this will look like it hasn't done anything. But if you scroll down, you see a list of recent blog posts and a View Blog link to access all the posts by that member.

To create your own blog, click the Blogs button, and then use the Create Blog button on the right-hand side. Enter the title of your blog post into the Subject box, and put the post itself into the Body box.

You then have two privacy settings: who is allowed to comment, and who is allowed to read your post. You can restrict blog reading and commenting to your friends if you wish. You can also ban commenting outright and limit your post's visibility to yourself. That's useful if you want to save a work in progress and come back to edit it later.

If you make your blog visible to everyone, anyone with Internet access can read your blog post, and could even find it through search engines. There's no option to have only Saga Zone members read your blog.

The calendar shows the birthdays of your Saga Zone friends in green if they have allowed their age to be shown on their profiles. You can also add private notes, which are only visible to you, using the link to the right of the month grid. That means you can use the calendar to keep track of your own social engagements and commitments too. These notes appear on the calendar in orange. Click the X next to each one if you want to remove it from the calendar again.

To create your own event, click the Add an Event link, in the right-hand column beside the month grid. You'll be given a one-page form to enter your event information. Your event title is limited to 20 characters, and it's a good idea to try to get the location and a short description into that (for example, "London theatre trip"), because this is what appears in the date box on the calendar.

You also need to provide the time and date, a description of the event, the venue, its street, town and postcode. The description is the place to put most of the details, including price, dress code, theme, reason for celebration, and so on.

When you're creating an event, you can also create a forum thread so that people can chat about what they'd like to get out of the event and let you know whether they're coming or not. There are different social events forums for each region, and you'll be asked which one your event belongs in. If the event itself has emerged from a forum discussion, you can link your event to the existing thread by copying the website address of the forum and pasting it into the event forum. It's much easier to create the forum at the same time as the event, though, so even if you only have provisional details, it's probably worth doing that and adding in more information as it becomes available.

Once you add your event, a dedicated page is created for it. If you entered the postcode, a map of its location appears on this page, as well as the description and other details you entered. Your event is added to the public calendar, and your discussion topic appears at the top of the relevant forum, where it should soon be spotted by the regulars.

Making friends on Saga Zone

Because Saga Zone encourages you to use nicknames, your real identity is relatively concealed. The People Search (found under Search on the white navbar) enables you to search by location, interests, gender and age, and is more about finding others who share your interests than it is about tracking down real-world friends. If you do know your friends are on Saga Zone, the best thing is to ask them by email for their display name, and then search for that on the site to track down their profile.

The link to send a friend request is in the first box on a member's profile. You receive a message to tell you when the request is accepted.

Whenever there's a new friend request or message for you, you see an alert flashing in the top right of the screen. You can click that to go straight to the messages in your Inbox.

When you log in, you can click Friends on the blue navbar to see who else is online and send a private message. You can also de-friend people here, if that is sadly necessary. The Blogs button provides a handy shortcut to your friends' blog posts too.

Whether you have a friend relationship with somebody or not, you can send them a private message using the link on their profile. It's a good idea to send an introductory message at the same time as a friend request if the reason for the request won't be obvious.

There's much more to see and do at Saga Zone. It also enables you to create and share photo albums, and runs themed photo competitions. There's a fun stock exchange game where you can gamble on fictional stocks too. Take a look around!

Managing your privacy

As you've already heard, much of the content on Saga Zone is available to non-members too, including blog posts, galleries, and most forums. You can decide how much of your profile information is available to members and the public, though.

If you go to edit your profile, there is an option to edit your account settings (also available through the white navbar, under About Me). From here you can tick or untick boxes to:

- Show when you're online (enabled by default).
- Show your gender on your profile.
- Show your age on your profile (and your birthday on your friends' calendars).
- Show your county on your profile (enabled by default).
- Make your profile public to the Internet.
- Allow users to search for you.

Saga Zone keeps your email address confidential. Any messages to you will be routed through the site. So you don't need to worry about getting unsolicited emails from strangers.

Summary

- Saga Zone is a social network exclusively for over-50s

- Your account must be approved before you can edit your profile or post in forums

- Forums enable discussions to take place on a wide range of subjects, over a long period of time

- The breadcrumb trail provides shortcuts to higher levels of the forum

- If you are replying to somebody else's comment, quote their post so that others can see your reply in context

- Your blog enables you to post diary entries and creative writing and receive feedback from the Saga Zone community

- Saga Zone enables chat and photo-sharing in clubs, and has a calendar for organising real-world social events

- Take care with your privacy: much of the content posted on Saga Zone is available to everyone

Brain training

As usual, let's refresh our memories with a quick quiz. Multiple right answers are allowed.

1. The breadcrumb trail says Forum index >> Interests and Hobbies >> Languages >> Polish. Which of these is true?

a) The discussion might be about cleaning furniture

b) The discussion is in the hobbies forum

c) There is a forum dedicated to languages

d) There are four forums on the site

2. To share a photo on Saga Zone, you can . . .

a) Upload it from your computer to a forum

b) Link to a picture on the Internet in a forum

c) Upload it from your computer to a club

d) Email it to the site hosts

3. You can use Saga Zone to organise a social event down the pub . . .

a) True

b) False

4. Your blog posts can be commented on by . . .

a) Your friends

b) All site members

c) Anybody, including non-members

d) People in the same clubs as you

5. You can upload videos from your computer to a Saga Zone forum . . .

a) True

b) False

Answers

Q1 – b and c   **Q2** – b and c   **Q3** – a   **Q4** – b (unless you restrict commenting to your friends)

Q5 – b

Networking with other seniors at Eons

Equipment needed: Access to a computer with an Internet connection and web browser (see Chapter 1), plus your own email address. Membership list if you'd like to create an online meeting place for a real-world organisation (optional).

Skills needed: Ability to use a web browser (see Appendix A); understanding of how to register and create an online profile (see Chapter 2).

Eons is dedicated to the baby boom generation, those born between 1946 and 1964, and aims to help them to get the most from life. The age limit is more of a guide than a rule, though, and the site provides a warm welcome to anybody over 13. Even so, most members are likely to have a generous fistful of candles on their next birthday cake.

The site has 700,000 members, making it the largest network focused primarily on the needs of more mature web users. Because it's headquartered in the USA, it's also the ideal starting point for tracking down friends there or making new ones.

The site's features include photo-sharing, group discussions and blogs, which enable you to share your thoughts and creative writing. The site also welcomes real-life groups who want to meet online using its tools. If you are a member of a horticulture society or tennis club, for example, you could create an invitation-only group using Eons for it to help members keep in touch between meetings.

You can preview Eons to decide whether you want to join before registering.

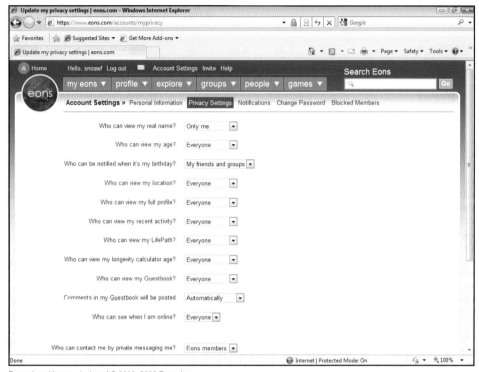

Reproduced by permission of © 2006–2009 Eons, Inc

Figure 7.2

emails here, and can also bunch up communications such as private messages, friend invites, and comments so that you receive them in a daily or weekly digest instead of in continuous dribs and drabs.

You can provide a middle or maiden name to help friends find you. In the Account Settings section, choose Personal Information from the local navbar and complete the box there.

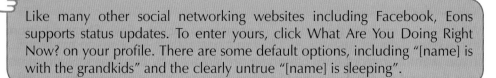

Like many other social networking websites including Facebook, Eons supports status updates. To enter yours, click What Are You Doing Right Now? on your profile. There are some default options, including "[name] is with the grandkids" and the clearly untrue "[name] is sleeping".

Uploading photos to your profile

If you want to share your holiday or just show off your new car, Eons enables you to add photos to your profile. Your photos are stored in your Photo Center, and are organised in folders. Your profile photos go into a Profile Photos folder, and there is a folder for your favourite photos.

To start adding photos, go to your profile and click Photo Center on the local navbar. Click the Add Photos link and you'll be asked to pick a folder for them to go into. You can choose to create a new album, in which case you need to provide a title, and description, and choose one of the options for who is allowed to see it, ranging from everyone, through friends and groups, to just yourself.

When you click the Choose Photos to Upload button, a file browser opens so you can select the photos from your computer.

You can choose more than one file from the same computer folder by holding down the Control (CTRL) key on the keyboard while you click once on each of the files you want. If you use the Shift key and click, you can select all the files between the first one selected and the last one.

Click the Open button when you're finished, and Eons starts uploading straight away.

If you want to assign a title and description to a photo, comment on it, or rotate it, navigate through your Photo Center folders to it and click it. You'll find options to do that in the menu at the top of the right column.

Finding friends on Eons

At Eons, you can use the same search engine to find people and to dig into the site's content. To get started, enter somebody's name in the Search box beside the main navbar. Press the Enter key or click the Go button to see the search results.

Within the search results, purple tabs enable you to fine-tune your search to concentrate on People, Groups, Blogs, and other site content. Click the People tab to see a list of those who match your search terms – like in Figure 7.3.

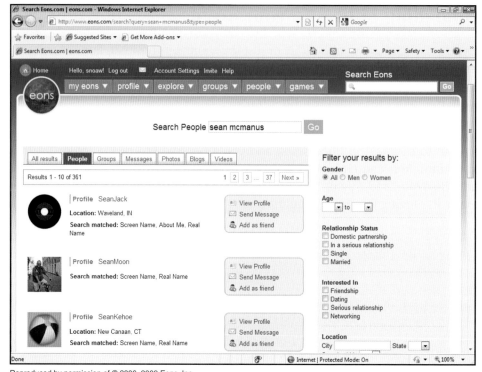

Reproduced by permission of © 2006–2009 Eons, Inc

Figure 7.3

You'll probably be overwhelmed with responses, so you can filter them by gender, age, and location using the options on the right. Eons suggests people in the order it thinks is a best match for who you want to find, but you can also sort results by how long people have been site members, and alphabetically by username. If you change any of the filter options, click on the green Filter button to refresh the results.

With so many people on the site, it can be difficult to track people down. If you already know somebody's email address or screen name on Eons, you get much better results if you enter it into the Search box.

There is a dedicated people search which you can find by choosing Search People from the pop-up menu that appears when you hover over People on the main navbar. If you then click Search for People I Know, you can narrow your search by name, screen name, or email address.

You can also add contacts from your webmail account (see Chapter 2) and can paste in a list of email addresses. To try that, click Invite above the main navbar.

Your own profile can help you find friends old and new, too: click your employers or favourite things, and Eons searches the site using those keywords so you can find others who share your interests or background.

Interacting with people on Eons

When you view somebody else's profile, it looks similar to your own. You can use the local navigation bar to view their groups, friends, photos, blogs, and guestbook, for example.

If you want to interact with someone, you have four options, which are in the rounded box beside their profile photo, as shown in Figure 7.4.

Reproduced by permission of © 2006–2009 Eons, Inc

Figure 7.4

You can:

- **Send a private message:** Your friend is notified of your message by email and Eons acts as go-between, shielding your email addresses from each other.

- **Write a comment:** Anything you enter here appears on the recipient's public guestbook.

- **Send a gift:** They do say it's the thought that counts, which is good because with virtual gifts, that's all you have! You can choose from a catalogue including new grandbaby cards, cakes, and smileys. A picture of your gift and your message appear on your friend's profile for two weeks. You can earn more gift credits by participating in groups, writing blogs, and posting comments.

- **Add as a friend:** A friend invitation is sent. If you receive one yourself, you'll be notified by email and when you log in. You can then click through to the sender's profile and find a link to accept the friend request in place of this Add a Friend link.

Note that members can restrict access to these features in their privacy settings, so if you don't see them it might be because they have been switched off.

Meeting other newcomers in groups

When you join Eons, you are automatically joined to a group for newcomers. There's a new group each month, so other members have a similar level of expertise to you. Don't worry though, you won't be left to stew together. Some more experienced members help out by answering your questions and providing tips on making the most of Eons.

There are several paths to your groups, but the quickest is to hover over Groups on the navbar, and in the pop-up menu, you'll see your group list at the bottom. Click the one you want to visit.

When you arrive at the group homepage, it looks like Figure 7.5.

As well as the latest messages, further down the screen you can see upcoming events for the group, which include members' birthdays. At the bottom, you can see a selection of the group's photos.

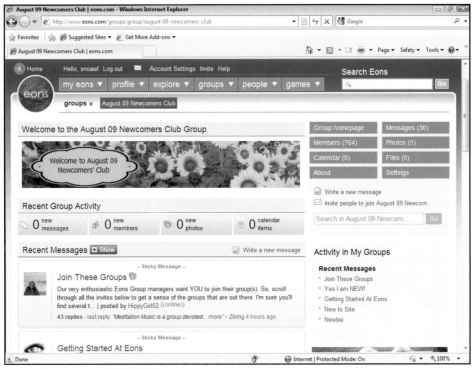

Reproduced by permission of © 2006–2009 Eons, Inc

Figure 7.5

The main navigation controls for the group are on the blue boxes at the top of the right-hand column. As well as messages and a calendar, which you'll learn about shortly, these links provide access to:

● **Group homepage:** Use this link if you get lost in the group and want to return to where you started.

● **Members:** You can see who else is in the group, and click through to their profiles.

● **Photos:** The photo albums for a group work in the same way as your profile photo albums.

● **Files:** Use this to upload and share files.

● **About:** An overview of the group.

● **Settings:** Use these to control how much email this group sends you.

The number in brackets after Members, Photos, and Messages indicates how many of them there are. So if it says Photos (5), it means five photos have been uploaded to the group. The calendar doesn't count birthdays for the purposes of this.

Responding to group messages

When you click Messages, the overview might look like a surrealists' convention, with all the posts completely unrelated to each other. That's because you're shown the top post in each thread in its entirety, but not the replies. If you want to see the replies to those posts, and dig deeper into the thread, you need to click the link at the foot of each post that says, for example, "42 Replies", or however many there are.

You can work through the replies using the page numbers at the top and bottom of the comments pages. When you get to the last page, you'll find a text box for your reply and a Post button to submit it.

Reply buttons on the messages overview page and on each page of comments whisk you to the end of a thread so you can comment straight away. Remember, it's good manners to read what others have said before you chip in with your own views.

If you want to start your own conversation, use the link that says Write a New Message, in the column on the right.

Using the group calendar

The group calendar can be a good way to tell group members about forthcoming shows and exhibitions that might interest them or to organise a meet-up for a private group of friends.

In the calendar, events are listed one after another, starting today and working into the future. You page through the events, similar to the way that you page through forum posts, using the Next button to go to the next page or clicking on a page number to jump ahead to it. There's no easy way to search for events in a particular month, so you need to guesstimate which page they might be on.

To add an event, click the link that says Add a Calendar Item on the right side. You need to provide the start and end dates and times, as well as a title and description for the event.

You can click the Publish button to add the event to the calendar straight away, or can use the Publish and Add Photo button if you'd like to add a picture from your computer or Photo Center first.

Your event will have its own page, where the description and photo appear, and members can leave comments, similar to the way they comment on messages.

Finding other groups to participate in

Eons has thousands of groups to explore, including over 700 about body and health, 1,400 about fun stuff, and over 700 dedicated to relationships. The groups are organised into categories, which include healthy living, games, hobbies, home and garden, sports, family, friends, pets, and romance.

To browse the directory of groups, hover over Groups on the navbar, and select Browse by Category from the menu that pops up. You can then click to enter one of the categories and see all the groups there. The busiest groups are shown first, but you can change the settings so that new groups or the largest groups appear first.

When you click a group, you can explore its members and messages and if you like what you see, click the Join this Group button on the group's homepage.

Creating your own group

If you want to create a group, you have two different options. You can create a group for Eons members, which can be public or only open to your invitees. You can also create a real-life group. This enables you to use Eons' infrastructure to create an online home for people you know in the real world, such as your local book club. In real-life groups, members use their real names instead of usernames which protect their identity.

It's a lot easier to join a thriving group than to start a new one, so search first to see if there's already a similar group you can participate in.

To start creating a group, select Create a Group from the Groups pop-up menu. First, you need to indicate whether you are creating a real-life group or a community group. Then you'll be shown a form to complete the relevant details. Whatever group type you're creating, you need to provide:

- **A group name:** This has to be unique if your group is a community group, and you can click the button to check availability, similar to the way you checked your screen name was not yet taken during registration.

- **A group description:** This appears on your group's homepage, About page, and in search results. Explain why the group exists and what its parameters are. If you're too vague here, it will be difficult to create a group with an identity.

- **Keywords:** These should be words that people searching for your group might use. Don't use commas to separate the words: just spaces. If you want to use a phrase, put speech marks around it.

If you're creating a community group, you also need to say which category it belongs in. If appropriate, you can provide a country for your group. You can decide whether to make your community group public (anyone can view or join), private (only members can view the group), or whether you'd like to strike a compromise of allowing anyone to view, but approving each request to join individually.

Of course, it's not a group until at least one more person joins, so the next step is to invite your friends. The interface for doing this is slightly different in real-life and community groups, but the functionality is broadly the same.

In community groups, click the Invite New Members button to see options to add people from your webmail account, enter email addresses manually, add your friends, or invite people by their Eons screen names. You will see something like Figure 7.6.

Whenever you enter email addresses using any of those options, they are added to the list on the right-hand side. The invitations aren't sent until you click Preview

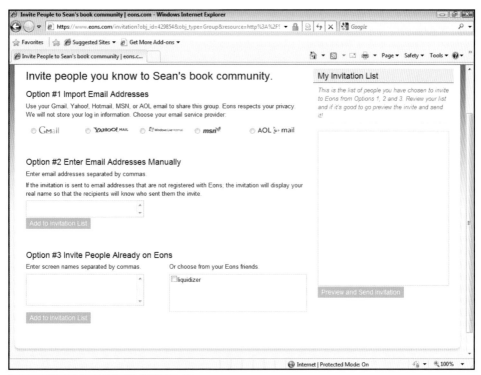

Figure 7.6

and Send Invitation, on the right. You'll be asked to add a personal message to go with the invitations.

If your group is a real-life group, the interface does much the same but looks completely different, as you can see in Figure 7.7.

Click Add From Your Email Address Book and you'll be taken to the familiar webmail sign-in form. The Add Manually link enables you to enter email addresses individually. Perhaps the most useful feature is to Upload a Spreadsheet. When you click that, you'll be given a link to download a blank spreadsheet to complete. You can then fill that out and upload it again. If you've already got a membership list for your club, you might find you can cut and paste the relevant columns into the Eons spreadsheet.

Once you've attracted some members, don't forget to get the ball rolling by starting some conversations. Like a good party host, you need to break the ice.

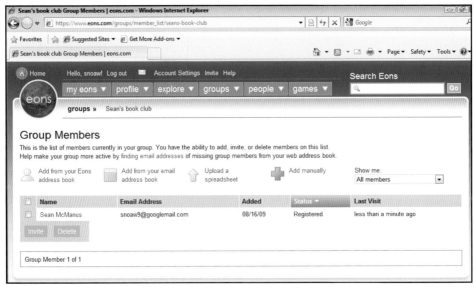

Reproduced by permission of © 2006–2009 Eons, Inc

Figure 7.7

When you own a group, the Settings option in its navigation (shown in Figure 7.5) is replaced with Manage Group. Click that, and you can add a photo banner to go across the top of the group's homepage, add guidelines, and edit the information you provided during creation.

Creating a blog

Your blog is the place on Eons where you can share your musings and writing. Readers can leave their comments, so a blog can be a catalyst for conversation. You can restrict each post to members of specific groups, everyone in your real-life groups, or your Eons friends. Alternatively, you can share it with the whole site or even non-members too.

Creating a blog is a doddle. Go into your profile, and select Blog from the local navbar. On the right, you'll see a link to write a blog post.

The blog form is similar to forms you've seen for creating forum posts and groups: you need to provide a blog title, the content itself (called the 'Entry'), keywords to help others find the post, and then indicate who you'd like to be able to see the post. You can add a photo before publication too.

Your blog posts appear on your profile, and your friends see them in their Recent Activity feed when they log in, unless you have blocked them from reading them.

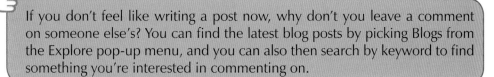

If you don't feel like writing a post now, why don't you leave a comment on someone else's? You can find the latest blog posts by picking Blogs from the Explore pop-up menu, and you can also then search by keyword to find something you're interested in commenting on.

Summary

- Eons is the largest network focused primarily on the needs of more mature web users

- Much of the content on Eons is available to the public. Your privacy settings enable you to restrict your information to yourself, your friends, or all Eons members

- You may upload 100MB of photos per month to your Photo Center

- Find your friends using search (by real name, Eons screen name, or email address), by adding email contacts, or by clicking shared places on your profile

- From a member's profile, you can send a private message, write a public comment, send a virtual gift, or send a friend request

- You are automatically joined to your month's newcomers group. Groups can share photos, files, messages, and events

- You can use Eons to create an online meeting place for a real-life group, such as your local tennis club

- You can write a blog to share your ideas with your friends, groups, all members, or everyone

Brain training

Check your understanding of Eons with these multiple choice questions. There might be more than one correct answer.

1. You must be over 50 to join Eons . . .

a) True

b) False

2. If you send a message through somebody's profile, the recipient will find out your email address . . .

a) True

b) False

3. Virtual gifts are . . .

a) Free

b) Delivered by post

c) Software that can be downloaded

d) Decorations for the recipient's profile

4. Members of Eons can see each other's real names . . .

a) Yes, all the time

b) Yes, if they're in the same groups

c) Yes, if they're in the same real-life groups

d) No, they can't

5. You can upload a spreadsheet of your friends to . . .

a) Your real-life group

b) Any group you're a member of

c) Your profile

d) Your Photo Center

Answers

Q1 – b   **Q2** – b   **Q3** – a and d   **Q4** – c

Q5 – a

Finding and planning real-world social events at Meetup

8

Equipment needed: Access to a computer with an Internet connection and web browser (see Chapter 1), plus your own email address. You will need a credit card if you plan to run your own group (optional).

Skills needed: Ability to use a web browser (see Appendix A); understanding of how to register and create your profile (see Chapter 2).

You've already seen how you can organise reunions and meetings using Facebook, Friends Reunited, and Saga Zone. Attending events can give you a chance to see old friends you've lost touch with, and cement your online friendships.

Meetup (**www.meetup.com**) takes a slightly different angle: whereas events are just one of the things that sites like Facebook offer to their communities, Meetup exists primarily to bring people together in the real world. It describes itself as a network of local groups, and says that over 2,000 groups meet in local communities each day thanks to its planning tools. The site's mission is to revitalise the local community and help people worldwide to organise themselves into groups.

The interests represented by groups are as varied as the people within them: near me I could mingle with chess players, poker players, kung fu movie makers, solo travellers, badminton players, readers, Agatha Christie fans, Chihuahuas (and their owners), jive dancers, and German speakers. There are also many groups dedicated to socialising, bringing people together just to make friends.

Because you can restrict membership of your group to those you know, Meetup is also a great way to create an online meeting place for an existing local community group. Meetup can help to sustain momentum between meetings, provide advanced planning tools, and even enable people to pay before they attend. Organising groups does incur a fee, but this can be passed on to members.

Finding Meetup groups near you

You can search for groups without having to register, so you can quickly see what's on offer in your community.

Go to **www.meetup.com** and you'll see a box to find a Meetup group near you. It contains a text box to enter your topic or interest, a pull-down menu to select your country, and a text box for your postcode. If you leave the topic box empty, you'll be shown all groups local to your postcode. If you choose a country that doesn't use postcodes, that box transforms to ask for the ZIP code or become a pull-down menu for choosing a city.

For each group in the search results, you can see its name, a short description, its distance away from you, the number of members, and the average rating that the group's previous gatherings have received. You can sort the results by the best match (which is the default), by distance, or by size of membership.

If you click a group's title or its picture in the search results, you'll be taken to its group homepage.

Exploring the group homepage

A group's homepage is its front door and welcome mat. This is where the group receives prospective and returning members, and gives them an overview of the group's activities. The homepage for a Meetup group looks like Figure 8.1.

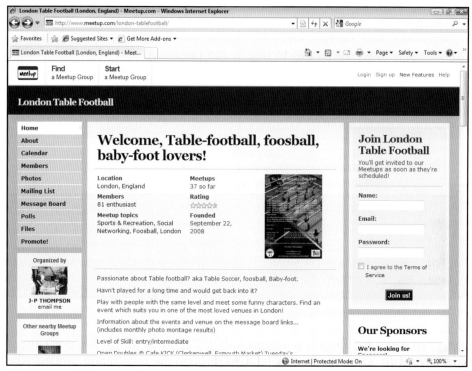

Figure 8.1

Group owners can customise the design so the colours might be different for your group, but the layout should be roughly the same.

The homepage for my table football group includes a summary of its goals (ahem), and details of how many members there are and how many meetings there have been. Each group can decide what it wants to call its members, so mine are listed as enthusiasts, but yours might be gardeners, singers, or something else.

Further down the page, you can find out where and when the next meeting is taking place, and how many have confirmed they're attending. Each meeting has its own summary too, explaining what will take place, any entry fees, and any other requirements you need to know about. Beside the list of upcoming meetups is a list of past gatherings. You can see when they took place, how many attended, and what the average rating was from attendees.

receive emails from organisers only or from everyone, and can choose to batch the discussion into a single daily digest instead of seeing it piecemeal in real time.

Planning to attend events

Now the main event: finding gatherings you want to attend and making plans to be there. It's natural to feel a bit nervous about trying new things and meeting new people, but there are fantastic opportunities on offer and there are usually others there who feel the same as you do.

To find your way back to your group, you can go through your profile or through your homepage, found by clicking on the site's logo in the top left corner.

You can then click Calendar on the left navbar of the group's homepage to see what's coming up this month. Meetup is all about face-to-face meetings, so the calendar is the heart of each group. The easiest way to browse events is to go into the calendar section on the left navbar, and then use the Upcoming tab. It lists all the forthcoming events on one screen, like Figure 8.3.

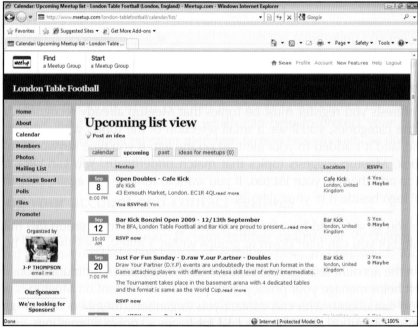

Figure 8.3

Beside each event you see its location and the number of people who intend to be there. If you click the Read More link at the end of the short description, you'll be shown the full event information on this page.

To help the organiser to plan the event, and to show other members that you'll be there, you should RSVP. Click the event box on the calendar or on the RSVP link in the upcoming list to go to the event's page.

Everything you need to know about the event is here, including who else is attending. To find out what the venue is like, click its name on the event page and a new window opens. Reviews from other Meetup members here tell you how noisy and how expensive the venue is.

At the top right of the event page is your reply box. The reply options vary depending on how the organiser has configured them, but typically you can answer the question "Will you be there?" with yes, no, or maybe. It obviously helps organisers to know that you're coming (or hoping to), but it also shows you're engaged with the group and interested in what they're doing if you politely decline. Often, the RSVP options allow you to bring guests and ask you to specify how many you'll have.

Your RSVP is shown on the event's page, so make sure you only add comments you're happy to be public. If you want to ask a private question of the organiser, you'll find a link to email him or her underneath the navbar on the left of the calendar pages. If you want to chat about the event with other attendees, you can leave a comment on its page.

These are mostly informal and often free events, but it's still good manners to turn up if you say you will and to let the organiser know if you can't make it after all. If your plans change, edit your RSVP. Go to the event's page, and in the top right you'll see your reply. Underneath, there's a link you click to say you've Changed Your Mind. Your RSVP status is also shown on your view of the group calendar and on the upcoming page.

To help find your way to the event, print a ticket incorporating a map from the group homepage. It includes the venue details and event agenda as a reminder of what you can look forward to. Have fun!

Meetup is a friendly community, but because you're meeting with strangers, you should take reasonable precautions. It's safest to meet at public venues, like pubs and restaurants, where there will be others around. Be careful about the personal information you give out, and consider taking a friend to your first meeting.

Keeping track of all your events and groups

To keep track of activity across all your groups, visit your homepage by clicking the site logo in the top left. This is also where you arrive when you first log in.

On this page, you'll see new members, new RSVPs, message board posts, photo uploads, and comments from across all your groups. If your homepage is too busy, you can hide some of the postings. Hover over one of the entries and a link appears on the right to hide all posts of that type (such as RSVPs) from that group. You can click Manage Feed to recover anything you hide by mistake.

There are links to take you into your groups here too, but the most useful feature is your personal calendar. This will show all the events from across all your groups, on a single calendar. Click the date to see the corresponding events summarised underneath. You can filter the calendar by RSVP status too, so that you only see those events you've committed to go to, or those where you haven't yet made a decision.

Sharing ideas for events

The most successful events are often shaped by the online community, with members submitting ideas and helping to define the agenda. Whether you've got a hot idea for something new, or want to reassure organisers that you're interested in their proposals, there are three main tools you can use to help plan events:

- **The message board:** On each topic page there is a discreet Add a Reply link at the top and bottom of the page. If you want to kick off a new thread, use the Start a New Discussion link at the top of all the message board pages. If you tick the box to track the discussion, Meetup sends you a daily email summary of any replies in it.

- **The mailing list:** All the conversation takes place on email using your usual email program or webmail. Each mailing list has its own email address, shown at the top right of the mailing list page. Whenever you send a message to this address, it is automatically forwarded by email to everyone in the group who is on the list. Some lists are moderated, which means the organiser must approve a message before it is sent. Sent messages are archived in the group's mailing list pages. Note that if you send a message to the list, everybody on the list is able to see your email address. Only organisers can delete messages from the archive.

- **Voting in polls:** When there's a new poll for you, you'll see a yellow warning triangle beside Polls on the navbar. After you've voted, the graph shows you the total of all votes so far.

You can find all of these through the navbar on the left of the group pages.

Don't use the mailing list to share attachments: they are automatically stripped out during moderation and on the digest versions of the list. Upload files instead to the group's files section.

Group organisers get to decide the what, where, when and how of all events, but members can also post ideas on the calendar. To post a new idea, go into the Ideas for Meetups tab within the group's calendar section. If there are existing ideas, you can show your support by ticking any that you like. If you've had a brainwave for a gathering, click the Post an Idea button and you can enter a short summary and more details. Organisers can turn these suggestions into events, or use them to inform their future planning.

Uploading photos to the group

When you go to a meetup, don't forget your camera! Groups can share their memories of great times by uploading photos to the group's photo albums.

To browse the photo gallery, click Photos on the group navbar. You start at the album that was most recently added to, but you can choose a different album from the list at the bottom right of the page. Figure 8.4 shows what an album looks like.

Figure 8.4

The first image is shown large, with a strip of small preview images (thumbnails) across the bottom. If you click one of those, it will appear as the main image. Underneath the thumbnail strip is a scrollbar you slide to the right to see more thumbnails if the album has more than five photos. The thumbnails obscure the main image, so if you want to hide them, click the Down Arrow button underneath the scrollbar.

If you prefer to let the computer do all the work (and why not? – that's what it's there for), click the Play button underneath the scrollbar and a slideshow displays all the photos in turn. Pay attention: it loops forever if you let it, so if you have a niggling feeling you've seen a photo before, you probably have.

To add photos, click the Add Photos link underneath the photo album title. As with Facebook (see Chapter 3), you need to install an add-on which streamlines photo uploading. Only group organisers can create albums, so you'll have to use the main group folder, or a more relevant folder created by the organiser.

> If the uploader doesn't work, or if you're using a public computer and you're not allowed to install it, there is a simple upload form. You have to upload each picture individually though, so it's much more time-consuming.

Uploading files to the group

If you've got a knitting pattern, song, or film to share, you can upload a file to your group. Click Files on the navbar and then click Add a File.

Your file can be a maximum of 10MB, but don't hog all the space: the group only has 100MB for everyone, so when a file is no longer needed, go back to the files section and click Delete to free up the space for others.

If you download files, don't forget to scan them for viruses. It's risky to install software obtained from a source like this. You can see who has uploaded it and use your common sense to work out how trustworthy you consider this person to be, but sometimes people upload files in good faith, unaware they contain viruses or spyware.

Creating and managing your own event group

If there isn't a group in your area catering to your interests, perhaps you could step up to organise your own. As you've already seen, Meetup members can register new groups they'd be interested in and when you create yours, anybody matching your topic and geography is notified that your group is starting up. There might already be hundreds of others waiting for you to start the ball rolling.

You can find out how many people are waiting for a group on a particular topic by going through the Find a Meetup group button, and then clicking More underneath one of the categories. The full list of topics within that category includes how many people are waiting for a group on each topic. This is a global total, so there's no way of knowing how many of them live near to you. It's a good indication, though: if 10,000 people are waiting for a group on your subject, and you live in a city, there's a good chance some of them are local. If only five people have so far expressed an interest, it's unlikely there's anyone local waiting. Don't let that stop you from opening the group, but don't expect overnight success, either.

Being a group organiser carries responsibilities and is far more time-consuming that just being a group member. You're the person who must decide what takes place when, must arrange the venues and travel where required, and must schedule the guest speakers. While you can appoint assistant organisers to help with (or even lead) most of your event planning, the group ultimately depends on you to manage the assistants and keep things running.

Your commitment isn't just time, either. Organisers are charged $19 per month (about £12), with rates dropping to $12 (about £7.50) per month if you prepay for six months. Your subscription enables you to run up to three separate groups, and you can charge members a fee to participate in the group or its events so you can reclaim the money if you wish.

The subscription plans are all supported by a 30-day money back guarantee. If you think you might be interested in running a group, you can try it out for a month risk-free.

To start setting up your group, click the Start a Meetup Group link at the top of the screen. The first form asks you for the group's location, name, and description. You can also customise the homepage headline (from Welcome!) and decide what group members are to be called (such as anglers, knitters, readers, or photographers).

You can customise the web address too, which will be **www.meetup.com/your-choice**. Meetup completes it with your group name automatically but if you edit it to include words that relate to your location and topic, you make it easier for potential members to find you through a search engine. Separate words with dashes, so you might have a web address like **www.meetup.com/ birmingham-uk-classical-music-fans**.

Before you click to the next page, you must tick the box to pledge to create a real, face-to-face community. It's up to you whether you stand and salute to take this oath.

You can list your group in up to seven topics. The more topics you provide, the more waiting members will be notified about your group, and the more places you appear in the Meetup directory. Don't be tempted to pick inappropriate groups to fill up the spaces though. Such behaviour can be seen as untrustworthy, which makes it hard to persuade members to join your group.

You have several slots to enter your topics on the left, with some suggested topics appearing on the right, as shown in Figure 8.5.

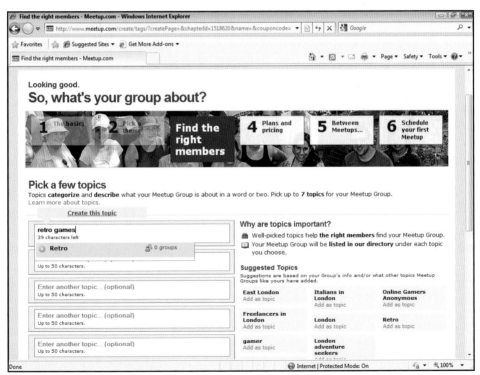

Figure 8.5

As you enter your topic, Meetup tries to complete it from the existing topics by showing you a list of matches underneath the text box. If your topic doesn't exist yet, you'll be given the option to create it. New topics have nobody waiting for them, so you might lose an opportunity to find members. In the longer term, you can make it easier for people to find you if the topic is genuinely missing, though. Use existing topics first, but don't be afraid to create new topics where needed and where you have slots available.

When you come to make your payment by credit card, remember to check that the connection is secure. Look for the padlock in your browser frame (not the web page content). Note that your credit card is automatically re-billed when your prepaid period expires. If you join using the monthly subscription fee, you'll be charged every month until you cancel.

After payment, you are asked to decide whether your group has a message board and/or mailing list. You are also asked to write a welcome email for new members. Use this to encourage them to participate in the group by sharing event ideas and most importantly by RSVPing to planned events.

Creating your first event

Members are more likely to join a group that has an event planned, so the final stage in creating your group is to schedule your first meeting. This isn't as hard as it sounds. Meetup suggests a title for your event and even proposes some venues that other site organisers have used. You can click a venue name for more information about it in a new window, including a map and reviews of those who attended past events there.

You can schedule events to repeat monthly or weekly if you like, so that you don't have to keep entering a regular event in the calendar.

If you don't want to create an event now, you can click the link to skip this stage at the top of the screen.

Fine-tuning your group settings

Don't panic: you won't receive an influx of enquiries straight away. Meetup gives you three days to get your house in order before it sends a message to waiting members to tell them about your group. On your group homepage, Meetup tells you how many people it will be announcing your group to, and how long you have before that happens, with a countdown measured in days, hours and minutes. It doesn't change unless you refresh the page or go to a different page and come back, so at least you don't have to watch your remaining preparation time slipping away.

As organiser of the group, you'll see a mini-navbar above the group's main navbar on the left side of the screen. This has options for scheduling meetings, emailing members, changing your group settings, and keeping track of the money.

The group creation has been accelerated by leaving out some of the configuration options, so your first stop should be the Group Settings option on the organiser navbar. This shows you an overview of all the different settings categories you can manage, and a summary of what's covered in each category.

From here, you can edit any of the information you provided during group creation. There are also several new options which you didn't see during setup:

- **Upload a group photo (found in the Basic Info settings):** You click the Browse button to open the file browser, pick a file, and then click the Submit button. The group photo appears on the group homepage and in search results.

- **Profile questions (found in the Your Members settings):** You can ask members up to five questions as they join, so you can do a spot of market research to find out what events will be most popular. Enter the question in the text box, and then click the Add Profile Question link for the next one. There are links to edit or delete a question beside it.

- **New member profile requirements (found in the Your Members settings):** Before allowing people to join, you can require them to complete an introduction, upload a profile photo, and/or answer the profile questions.

- **Communications options (found in the Optional Features settings):** Here, you can choose to moderate all messages on your mailing list before they are sent. This page also lets you specify the default currency and what will be included in the What's New? section of your group homepage.

Sharing the load

You can appoint group members to be assistant organisers, so they share much of the work of keeping the group going. To do this, click Members on the navbar and beside the appropriate member, click the link to Make Assistant Organiser. Assistant organisers can do all the day-to-day group management activities, including managing events, members, photos, and message board discussions.

A final word

How did we do at the table football? It depends how you look at it. On the pitch, we lost: the tournament had five games and we only won one of them. But, overall we won: we had a fantastic evening, got to see some championship table football skills, and tried something new that we might not otherwise have discovered.

My first table football meetup was a good example of what Meetup can do for you. It can introduce you to new pastimes under expert guidance, and give you a chance to meet new people in a friendly environment. Social networking isn't always about sitting in front of a PC.

Summary

- Meetup helps you to find real-world events to attend near you, and to organise your own

- Organisers must pay a monthly fee, but can pass this on to members through subscription fees or in the cost of events

- You should keep your RSVPs up to date to help organisers plan and to encourage them even if you can't attend

- Members can discuss event ideas on the message board or mailing list, and can vote in polls and post event ideas on the calendar

- Photos and files can be uploaded for sharing within the group

- If there isn't a group for your interests, you can create your own

- The money management tools enable you to keep track of your group's profit or loss, and provide transparency to paying members

- Organisers are responsible for planning all events, but you can appoint an assistant to help

Brain training

Time for a spot of revision! You can choose more than one right answer for these questions. Good luck.

1. Meetup is a good site to use if you want to . . .

a) Chat online about cats

b) Find a five-a-side football team to play in

c) Organise your local amateur dramatic group online

d) Make virtual friends on the other side of the world

2. The cost of joining a group . . .

a) Is nothing

b) Depends on the costs of operating the group

c) Depends on how much (if anything) the organiser charges for group membership

d) Goes to Meetup

3. You should update your RSVP to events . . .

a) Only if you're certain you can go

b) Whether you can go or not

c) Only if you're taking others with you

d) If you wanted to go, but can't now

4. As an ordinary group member, you can help to plan events by . . .

a) Scheduling them on the calendar

b) Proposing ideas on the calendar

c) Participating in votes

d) Discussing plans by email using the mailing list

5. As group organiser, you can encourage members to support your group financially by . . .

a) Staging some successful events first

b) Making your accounts transparent, so they can see where the money goes

c) Keeping group membership free and including the Meetup costs in the event fees

d) Begging them

Answers

Q1 – b and c   **Q2** – c   **Q3** – b and d   **Q4** – b, c and d

Q5 – a, b and c. Hopefully d won't be necessary!

Creating your own social network at Ning

9

Equipment needed: Access to a computer with an Internet connection and web browser (see Chapter 1), plus your own email address.

Skills needed: Ability to use a web browser (see Appendix A); understanding of how to register and create your profile (see Chapter 2).

Wouldn't it be great if you could have your own social network, just for you and your friends? It would certainly beat squatting on somebody else's network, turning a blind eye to the features you don't want and having pretty much the same experience as everybody else who uses that network.

Ning (**www.ning.com**) makes it easy to create your own social network. You choose which features your network uses, including blogs, chat, groups, events, photos, videos, and music. Features you don't need won't clutter up your screen, and you can extend the functionality with third-party content and applications. It's your group, so you decide who joins and what the rules are.

Ning is free, so the only limitation is your imagination. You could create a group to keep in touch with the extended family, sharing photos, videos, and chatting

As you learned on Eons (Chapter 7), you can choose multiple files from the same folder by holding down the Control (CTRL) key on the keyboard while you click once on each of the files you want. If you use the Shift key and click, you can highlight all the files between the first one selected and the last one.

If you thought it responded quickly, it's because the photos haven't uploaded yet. The photo upload box now shows the filenames of all the photos you want to upload, as you can see in Figure 9.5. If you want to add more, perhaps from a different folder on your PC, click the Add More link at the bottom left. If you've changed your mind about a picture, click the green cross to its right to delete it.

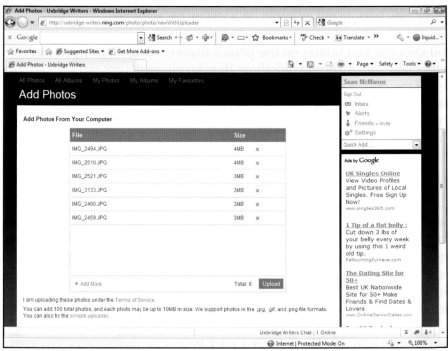

Reproduced by permission of Ning, Inc

Figure 9.5

Once you're happy with your list of photos, click the Upload button on the bottom right of the photo upload box. You can add a maximum of 100 photos and each one can have a file size of up to 10MB, which is more than twice the size of a typical good-quality digital photo.

As each photo uploads, you can watch its progress bar stretch from left to right. Or, and this is my preferred option, you can put the kettle on. It'll take a while if you have more than a couple of photos to upload.

If you can't get the photo uploader to work, try the simple uploader instead. The link is underneath the bulk photo uploader. You'll need to browse for each photo individually, and can only upload eight at a time. Ning will remember your choice next time you go into the photos section, so if you want to try the bulk uploader again, click on the link at the top of the basic uploader form to switch back.

Once the photos have uploaded, it's time to organise them, as you can see in Figure 9.6.

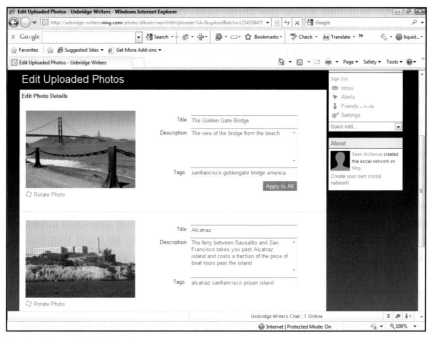

Reproduced by permission of Ning, Inc

Figure 9.6

Tags only work within the section you're viewing. So when you click a tag in the photos section it won't show you any videos that share that tag, and vice versa. To search across the whole network for a tag, use the Search box at the top right of the screen, as shown in Figure 9.4.

Your video won't appear in your network's video section until it's been converted to Ning's standard format, which can take 5 minutes or more. If you want to edit its details in the meantime, you can still find it by clicking Videos on the network's navbar and then clicking My Videos underneath it.

Ning also enables you to post content from popular video-sharing site YouTube. Find the video you want to share on YouTube and navigate to the screen where it plays. Go to the address bar here (tap F6), highlight the URL (CTRL+A), and copy it to the clipboard (CTRL+C). Return to your Ning network and go to Add a Video, but instead of browsing for a video on your computer, click the YouTube logo at the bottom of the page. You can then paste (CTRL+V) the web address from YouTube into the form. Ning retrieves the video's description and title automatically, and gives you a chance to tag it before clicking Save to publish it to the network. YouTube videos don't need to be converted, so they appear instantly in the videos section of the network as well as in your My Videos section.

Members can also add up to 100 music and spoken word recordings in the popular MP3 format. Each one can be 20MB, which is roughly 20 minutes at a good audio quality. The upload process is similar to that for videos and photos, but audio does not appear on the navbar. Members have an audio box on their profile pages, and the organiser can edit the one on the main page.

Adding blog posts

As you've seen on other sites, including Saga Zone (Chapter 6) and Eons (Chapter 7), blogs are a great way to kick off a discussion. To get started, click Blogs on the navbar and then click the link on the right to Add a Blog post.

Think of your title as your headline, and make it enticing. The entry box is where you type your blog post.

You can add tags, choose a date and time for it to go live, and edit the privacy options for who can view it and comment on it. When you've finished, click the Preview button to check it looks okay, and then click to Publish Post. If you want to save a work in progress, click Save As Draft.

In the network's blog section you can see all the blogs members have contributed, and can add your comments to them. Each member's profile (found by clicking their name against any of their content, or through Members on the navbar) also shows their blog posts. You can jump to your own by clicking My Blog at the top of the blogs section of the site.

Organisers can draw attention to the best blog posts by featuring them, similarly to how photos can be featured.

The Notes feature is only available to organisers and is used for posting important notices on the main page. There are more advanced formatting options available, but this otherwise works in much the same way as the blog.

Adding events

Your social network can have its own events calendar, to which any members can add an event. The events section of the site lists upcoming events and has a link to Add an Event.

The form to add a new event is similar to those you've used on Facebook, Saga Zone, and other sites. You provide an event title, description, type (such as 'party'), date, and location. You can restrict events to invitees only, or open them up to anyone who wants to attend. You also decide whether the guest list is published or not.

After you add an event, you are given the option to invite people from your webmail address book or by entering email addresses. You can also invite all members of the network or your friends within it. If you don't want to invite anyone, click the Skip link craftily hidden underneath the event summary on this screen.

Members can RSVP from the event's page, which is found through the list of upcoming events. Once they have replied, they can also add comments to the event's page.

> Use the Quick Add pull-down from the top box in the right-hand column to save time. It provides one-click access to the posting feature for photos, videos, music, blog posts, and events.

Communicating with people in your network

One of the reasons that Ning is such a great tool for building a social network is that its communications features are similar to those on other websites. It means they feel intuitive, and members don't have to go through a lengthy learning process to begin networking.

Like Facebook, Saga Zone, and many other sites, Ning enables members to form friend relationships. The main benefit of making friends on Ning is that it enables finer privacy control because you can restrict your content to your friends. It also makes it easier to find your friends' profiles, through the Friends page link in the column on the right. You won't be automatically notified of your friends' updates on the site, though, in the way that you are (constantly) on Facebook.

The person-to-person messaging options are similar to Facebook and are found on each member's profile. If you want to send a private communication, use Send a Message. You can also comment on the member's wall to add a public message to their profile. If you're told that the member is moderating comments, your message won't appear on their profile until they've approved it.

The chat system on Ning can be found on the homepage and is also accessible from the navbar. It is similar to the Chatterbox on Saga Zone, and Group Chat on Friends Reunited. The Chat window (see Figure 9.7) is split into three panes: on the left, the conversation; on the right, the list of online members; and at the bottom, the text entry box. When you type a message into the entry box and press the Enter key, your text is moved into the conversation box, where it can be seen by everyone. Other online members can chip in on the conversation at any time. This is a good place for a natter, but not the place to go if your conversation archive might be useful in future because chat contents are automatically deleted after the conversation has come to an end.

Figure 9.7

You can chat privately with a member, too. Click on their name in the list of online members and an option appears to chat privately. When you click it, a new chat tab opens with that person's name at the top of it (shown with the tab for Fred Jones in Figure 9.7). You can hop between the private and public (main) chats by clicking their tabs. Just don't go talking about the others behind their backs!

Ning has a forum feature, which brings more permanence to conversations and enables them to take place over a period of weeks or longer. Anybody can add a discussion, and as group organiser it's a good idea to ignite debate and stimulate discussion by posting two or three to start things off. If you're short of ideas, ask members what they want to get out of the group.

When you add a discussion, you give it a title, add the meat of your message using the same formatting as used for blogs, and then add tags. You can also attach up to three files to the post. If you start a discussion, you can edit the first post at any time, but comments can only be edited by their creator for up to 15 seconds after they've been posted. Once a conversation runs out of steam, its creator can close it to stop any further replies being added.

When you take part in a forum discussion, you'll be automatically notified of any updates by email and you can find all your discussions in the 'my discussions' section of the forum.

If your network is tightly defined, you should find that the forums and chat are all you need. However, if your network represents a wide range of interests, you might find the discussion and membership becomes fragmented. The Groups feature enables members to create groups within your social network that have their own comments, forum, text boxes, and RSS feeds. Groups can have moderated membership, so they can be restricted to certain members. In most cases, adding groups brings a level of complexity you don't need. Some organisations have a natural fit, though, such as a national society that wants separate groups for each region. I recommend you use groups to simplify things when it becomes obvious how they will help you, but don't bother with them until then.

The chat depends on people being online at the same time. To take luck and coincidence out of the equation, why not schedule a regular chat session, so that members can all plan to be online at that time? You can publicise this on the calendar, in the forum, by adding a note to the homepage, and by sending an all-members message.

Managing your network

Most social networks and groups online are friendly and people get along great. Once in a while there is friction between members. Sometimes it's created deliberately, when a so-called troll stirs up trouble by writing posts designed to annoy. Other times, there can be a clash of personalities that spills over into name-calling or other inappropriate behaviour (a 'flame war'). Occasionally, people post content that they shouldn't, such as music from their CD collection.

Communities tend to be good at policing themselves. More often than not, a troll waddles in, posts something inflammatory, and is then roundly ignored by everyone, so he just wanders off again. Sometimes a member posts something they shouldn't, another member steps in to say they're out of line, and the whole thing is resolved amicably in minutes.

As the network owner, you will occasionally be required to step in and set things straight again, though. You're ultimately responsible for keeping the community running smoothly: you are its government, judge, and jury.

Your ultimate sanction is to ban members. As the organiser, when you click through to a member's profile, you have an admin option to ban them. Consider this a last resort and try to work with the member first to explain the community's expectations of how members behave.

If you want to, you can choose to approve members' content before it goes live (known as moderating it). It's better to rein in any control freak instincts you have for a number of reasons, though. For a start, if you have to read everything, you become a bottleneck. The amount of time you have available to approve content will restrict how lively and timely your network can be. Members generally know what's acceptable and reasonable, so reading everything is a lot of pointless work to catch the occasional lapse in standards.

If somebody does bring content to your attention that breaches the community's expectations, you can remove it then and guide its author to ensure that it doesn't happen again. Navigate to the problem content and you can delete it, or edit its title and tags. You cannot edit blog body content or media descriptions, because that might result in your views being misattributed to the content's original creator. If the problem is in these areas, give the member an opportunity to fix it themselves before you delete anything.

If you do want to screen content before publication, click Manage on the navbar and then click Feature Controls. From here, you can choose to approve blog posts, photos, events, groups, and videos. You can also enable or disable features such as status updates, theme customisation on members' pages, and searching by age here.

Moderation works best when applied with a light touch, and when the rules are clear and consistent. Don't confuse your moderation privileges with your right to reply: if you don't like something, use the comments. If the community needs to be protected from something, that's the time to intervene as moderator.

> Only a network's organiser will see Manage on the navbar. It's also the place to go if you want to change anything you configured during setup (such as the layout, appearance, or network privacy), or if you want to broadcast a message to all your members.

Managing your privacy

Ning provides each member with a lot of control over who can see their content and comment on it. At the top of the right-hand column is a box with your name in it, which includes a link to your settings (see Figure 9.4).

Behind this link, your settings are divided into four sections, accessed using links on the left:

● **Profile:** For editing your photo, email address, password, name, birthday, gender, and country; and for resigning from the network.

● **Privacy:** Enables you to restrict your profile page to your friends list, limit content you upload to friends or yourself, and restrict your events to just your friends or yourself. You can also control who can see comments from others on your content and can choose to approve blog and profile comments before they go live. There are options to decide what goes into your latest activity box too.

● **Email:** To control when Ning sends you an email update or alert.

● **My Page:** Enables you to control the appearance and URL of your profile page.

In each section, you must click the Save button at the bottom to apply your changes.

Unless the network is a private network, your content will mostly be available to anyone (including non-members) unless you change your privacy settings. The only exception is your profile, which is available to all network members by default.

Your privacy settings only affect content that is uploaded from that point on. If you say your photos should be visible only to you, this won't hide photos that were previously added to the network. To change the privacy settings for a particular content item, click its Edit link.

Each Ning-powered network has its own privacy settings. So, if you're in two networks that use a Ning ID, you'll have to change your privacy settings in each one separately.

Summary

- Ning enables you to create your own social network, and customise its features and design

- To create a successful network, be clear about its intended audience and areas of interest

- Pick a short web address that includes some descriptive keywords, so people can find your group through search engines

- As you customise your network, make sure that pages remain easy to read and use

- Your network can be used to share photos, videos, blogs, and events

- Members can leave public comments on each other's profiles, send private messages, and form friend relationships

- Chat enables all members online to communicate in real time. Members can also enter private chats one-to-one

- The forums enable longer-term discussions between members who are online at different times

- Network owners can police content and members, but it's better not to intervene unless absolutely necessary

- Most Ning content is available to the public. Edit your privacy settings to restrict who can see your content

Brain training

Test your network-building skills with this quiz. There might be multiple right answers.

1. A bad network definition would be . . .

a) Life, the universe and everything – all welcome to chat about anything

b) Ski enthusiasts – let's improve together

c) Manchester mothers – for advice, support and friendship

d) The Smith family – helping us to keep up with each other!

2. When customising your network's appearance, you should . . .

a) Use as many colours as possible

b) Make the writing as small as possible, so you can fit more on screen

c) Make sure the foreground and background colours have strong contrast, and text is easily readable

d) Stick to the default themes provided

3. To add a photo to your main page, you can . . .

a) Click the Edit button on the photo box title bar

b) Click the Add Photos link on the photo box on the main page

c) Go through Photos on the navbar and then click Add Photos

d) Use the Quick Add menu in the column on the right

4. If a photo is tagged . . .

a) Others can find it more easily

b) Members can use the tag to find related blogs and videos

c) The network organiser can edit the tags

d) That photo is 'it' and must chase other photos and tag them

5. If somebody writes a blog post about the election that you don't agree with, you should . . .

a) Comment on the blog post

b) Ban the member

c) Edit the blog post

d) Edit the blog's title or tags

Answers

Q1 – a   **Q2** – d and/or c   **Q3** – b, c and d   **Q4** – a and c

Q5 – a

PART IV
Appendices and Index

It's amazing. At the click of a mouse, he transforms into a muscular, suntanned, golden-haired Greek god.

Appendix: How to use your web browser

Equipment needed: Access to a computer with an Internet connection and a web browser, such as Internet Explorer or Safari.

Skills needed: Some familiarity with the computer, including the ability to find and run programs.

One of the great things about social networking is that it mostly takes place using your web browser. That means you can log in from any computer and have all your data and friends available to you. It also means you don't need to install any software, and you probably already have most of the skills you'll need.

This appendix explains how to get the best from your browser, so that you can easily use the social networking websites in this book. If you're the kind of person who already does all the Christmas shopping online, or who follows the football headlines on the Internet, you will already have the skills required for social networking. But this appendix will also introduce you to some advanced features of your browser, which you might not know about yet.

What is a web browser?

Your web browser is the program that enables you to undertake all the activities of the World Wide Web, the most popular part of the Internet. Using your web browser, you can connect to your bank, an online store or an organisation like the BBC for the latest news and weather. Most companies are online today, but there is also a vast wealth of knowledge and entertainment that private individuals have put on the Web. Websites (also sometimes called 'sites') are destinations on the Internet: they are places you can access articles and photos, places you can browse and shop, and places where you can watch films or listen to music.

In the early days of the Web, using it was a passive affair: like TV or radio, all the information travelled one way. Today's websites are more sophisticated and interactive, and social networking websites are at the forefront of innovation. They provide a hub where you can meet with your friends and socialise, and enable you to publish your own content on the Internet for access by your friends or by the world at large.

Through your choice of network, and through the use of any privacy controls it provides, you decide who can access your information. Social networks are the tools, but you decide how you will use them.

Your web browser is the program that enables you to visit websites. If you're using Microsoft Windows, it is most likely to be Internet Explorer, which is by far the most popular browser. There is also a browser made by Apple, called Safari, and by Google, called Chrome, as well as two independent browsers called Opera and Firefox. They're all free, but you only need one, so just use whatever's already installed.

This chapter uses Internet Explorer as an example, but if you're using a different browser, don't worry. The features are largely the same, although the buttons and controls might look different and be in different places.

The first web browser was Mosaic, released in 1993. By making it easy to view and navigate content, Mosaic broadened the appeal of the Web beyond academia. Within a few years, businesses started to go online (Amazon launched in 1995), and the Internet began to arrive in the home.

Taking a tour of your browser

Start your browser. If you're using Internet Explorer, you should see an icon for this on your desktop or in your start menu. It looks like a blue lower case 'e', with a Saturn-style ring around it. When you open your browser, it starts to download your start page, which means it copies it to your computer from the Internet.

Your web browser is one of the simplest programs you'll ever use. There are thirteen main controls you need to know about, which is nothing compared to programs like Word or Excel. Here they are in Figure A1:

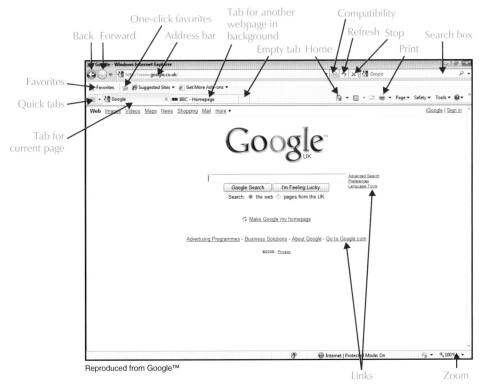

Figure A1

This screenshot shows the Google search engine (**www.google.com**), which is used to find other websites that have content you're looking for. When you open your browser, you'll probably see a different website at first, but don't worry about this for now. Concentrate instead on the blue area at the top of the screen. These are your browser controls. The most important ones are:

- **Address bar:** This is where you type in the address of the website you'd like to visit. As you navigate through pages, you'll see this bar change because every page on a website has its own unique address, also known as a URL. You can try it now by clicking on the address bar and then entering another address, such as **www.bbc.co.uk** for the BBC or **www.tesco.com** for Tesco. If you start typing a web address similar to one you've used before, the browser will suggest it so that you can click on it instead of having to type the rest of it. Web addresses always start with http:// or https:// (for a secure site) but the browser adds that for you automatically.

- **Back button:** Probably the most important button of all! Click this to go back, one page for each time you click it. If it's not working, it's probably because a link opened up in a new window. If you close that window, you should find your old session is still there in the original window you were using.

- **Forward button:** Use this button to go forward again after you've used the back button.

- **Refresh button:** click this to update the current webpage. This is useful for pages that change continuously.

- **Stop button:** use this to cancel downloading a page.

- **Print:** If you click this button, the webpage begins to print instantly, not always what you want. Click the triangle to the right of the printer and you can choose to preview the page first or set up your printer.

- **Search box:** You can type a subject in here to search the Web for webpages about it.

Those buttons are the gears and steering wheel, but there are some features that provide satnav, making it easier to get to the places you want to visit, and helping you to travel more quickly. Here are the highlights, which are also indicated on the previous screenshot:

- **Favorites:** Since the software is American, this feature is spelled that way. This button enables you to bookmark your favourite webpages, so you don't have to type their address in when you want to visit them again. Click this button to open your favorites, which include any defaults provided by your computer manufacturer as well as any you've added. You can click these to go straight to the related webpage. After clicking the Favorites button, you can also click Add to Favorites to bookmark the current webpage, either in an existing folder, or in a new folder you create. The Favorites button also enables you to view your history of visited websites under the History tab.

- **One-click favorites button:** If you click this, a button to visit the current webpage is added immediately to the right of the button. This makes it easy to visit your regular online haunts in a single click. To get rid of a button again, right-click it and select delete.

- **Home:** This takes you to your browser's start page. The default probably isn't too helpful but you can change this to whatever you want so that you see the football news first thing or go straight into Facebook, for example. To do this, visit the page you'd like to start at and then go through the browser's Tools menu (on the right hand side), and select Internet Options. In the Home page section at the top, click Use Current and then click OK. Whenever you open your browser in future, it starts at whatever webpage you're looking at now.

- **Empty tab:** The browser uses a filing cabinet metaphor for organising different websites you're using at the same time. You can select which webpage you want to see by clicking on the tab that sticks out the top of it. To open a new tab, click the empty tab. You can then enter a new website address into its address bar. To close a tab, just click it and then click the X that appears on the right side of the tab.

- **Quick tabs button:** If you have more than one tab open, click this to see a screenshot of all the current tabs at once. You can close any you don't need any more by clicking the X above them.

- **Compatibility button:** If the text on a website overlaps or it otherwise doesn't look right, try clicking this button. It tries to interpret webpages that don't work because they haven't had their design updated for the latest browser version. You only need to click once for each website; the browser remembers your setting. When compatibility mode is active, this icon goes blue.

Navigating websites

When you're out walking somewhere unfamiliar you sometimes just make up your route as you go along. Perhaps you'll see a sign to a river, and take a diversion along a different path to visit it. Or maybe you'll see a sign for a short cut, so you'll take that instead of retracing your steps home.

Navigating the Web is similar in that you find your way around it by surfing from webpage to webpage, following the signs. The signs, though, are called 'links'. They form a connection from one webpage to another, so you can travel to a new webpage by clicking the link. Sometimes a linked webpage might be in a different part of the same website, and other times it is independent and unrelated, part of a different website completely.

The easiest links to spot are blue underlined text, which make up a large part of the Google homepage shown in Figure A1. If you click Language Tools, for example, you'll be taken to a page of tools for translation and searching in foreign languages.

Sometimes links change colour, to tell you that the page behind them is one you've been to already. If you click Language Tools and then go back again, you'll see the link has changed from blue to purple. Unfortunately those default colours can be hard to tell apart. There is a reason we don't use blue and purple on our traffic lights.

Links can be anything, though: the text isn't always underlined, and even pictures can be links. If the website's well designed, the links should be obvious at a glance. If not, you can check whether something is a link by moving your mouse over it. If your cursor turns into a hand, it's a link. You'll see its destination URL in the bottom left of the browser.

Take a look at the shopping site Amazon shown in Figure A2.

If you'd like to go there yourself to try this out, just click in the address bar and type in www.amazon.co.uk and then press the Enter key on your keyboard.

Amazon uses blue underlined text for some of its links, but it also uses images to help you navigate. You can click any of the product images, and can click the basket picture in the top right to see what you're in the process of buying.

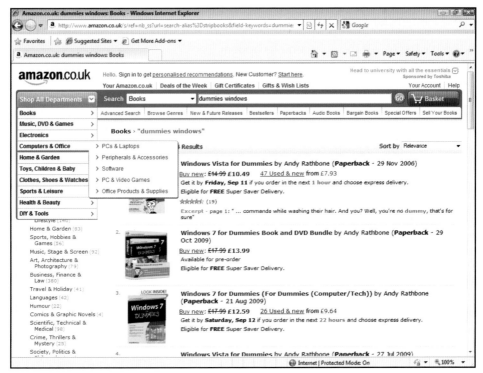

Reproduced by permission of Amazon.com, Inc

Figure A2

Lots of websites, including Amazon, have a logo in the top left to take you to the homepage, which is the main welcome page on the website. If you get lost, try clicking the logo in the top left to go back to the main entrance.

The main collection of links for getting around a website is known as a navigation bar, or navbar for short. Sometimes navbars change from screen to screen, but usually they're consistent across the whole website, so you can more easily learn how to use the website. Each site designs its own navbar, so they all look different, but they usually run across the top of the screen or down the left-hand side.

Down the left hand side of the Amazon site is a list of all the different departments. When you hover the mouse cursor over one of them, some options pop out on the right, which you can then click, as shown in the screenshot in Figure A2. This is known as a pop-up menu and enables the website to provide lots of options for getting about the site without having to fill up the screen with all the links at once. It's a widely used navigation technique, but sometimes you need to click on the navbar to get the submenu to appear.

If you're transferring a lot of data, such as a large photograph, you'll see a progress bar bubble away at the bottom of the screen. The green magma flows from left to right slowly, like a horizontal bar chart representing how much has downloaded so far. You can easily multitask so you don't have to sit around waiting for a download. If you hold down the control key while you click a link, it'll open in a new tab so you can carry on reading the current page while the next one loads in the background.

On the right side, you'll see a scrollbar. You've probably seen these used in office applications before; you click the bar, hold down the mouse button and slide the bar down the screen. It then scrolls the page so you can see what doesn't fit on the screen at the moment. If your mouse has a scroll wheel between its buttons, you can just click an empty area at the top of the browser and then roll the scrollwheel to move the page up and down.

In this book, the screenshots will be scrolled and zoomed in to show you as much useful content as possible. Sometimes the navbar is scrolled off the top of the screen, for example. If your screen looks different to the screenshot, try scrolling down first.

Using forms

Both the Google and Amazon websites use forms. These enable you to put your own information into the website, and play an important part in social networking.

On Google, for example, you can click the text box, type something you're interested in there, and then click the Google Search button. On the Amazon website, you can click the empty box at the top of the screen, enter what you want to buy, and then click the round Go button to find relevant products.

Figure A3 is an overview of some of the most common controls you'll come across, together with an example of how they might be used:

A quick overview of form controls

You can type freely into a box like this, until it stops accepting your input.
What is your name?
Sean McManus

Sometimes you can get textboxes that accept multiple lines.
What is your address?
My house,
In the middle of my street,
London

You can only select one radio button at a time.
Are you..?
⦿ Male
○ Female

You can select multiple tickboxes at once.
Do you like eating..?
☑ Chinese food
☐ Curries
☑ Salads
☐ Ice creams

For a pulldown menu, you have to click to open it. You can usually only select one option.
What is your home country? England ▾
England
Ireland
Scotland
Wales

Click on buttons to submit a form, or to carry out another action.
Submit   Clear form

Visit www.sean.co.uk to try these form controls out for yourself

Figure A3

The forms sometimes look a bit different on different social networking sites. The buttons in particular are often redesigned. The most important thing to note is that you can only choose one option using radio buttons (the round ones), can choose multiple options using tickboxes, and have to click to open the options on a pulldown menu.

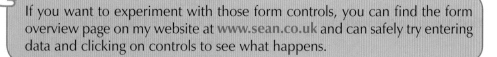

If you want to experiment with those form controls, you can find the form overview page on my website at **www.sean.co.uk** and can safely try entering data and clicking on controls to see what happens.

Appendix: Site directory

Now that you're an expert on social networking, why not see what other sites are out there? You can use your experience creating profiles, finding friends and groups, and sharing your photos, words and wisdom.

This directory outlines some of the key sites dedicated to different interests. It couldn't possibly be exhaustive: there are hundreds of networks out there. I've focused on those that add something different to the networks you've already read about in the body of this book, and I've focused on those that will provide a good welcome for older and wiser web users.

At the end of this directory, I've added a section about a website that can help you to cut the complexity of participating in several different social networks.

If there isn't a network here to tickle your fancy, you can often find groups dedicated to interests like these at major social networks including Facebook (see Chapter 3), Meetup (Chapter 13) and Ning (Chapter 15).

Biography

43things.com

While many social networks help you share the details of daily life, 43Things is a place to take a step back and think about the bigger picture: what you are doing with your life, and what you want to do next. It's where you share your life goals and receive support from others with similar aims. And as a member of the older and wiser generation, it's where you can share your past achievements and advise others who aspire to achieve similar goals.

At 43Things everybody publishes a to-do list of things they want to achieve. You're allowed to have any number of things on your list, up to a maximum of 43. Nobody knows why the limit is 43; it's just a quirk of the website. As you make progress towards your goals, you can write about it on the site and seek advice from others on the next steps.

Visits to 43Things are inspiring. The site is full of people who are passionate about self-improvement, and about getting the best out of life. There are plenty of ideas for things that will make life simpler, more exciting, and more rewarding. People of all ages mingle on the site, from students who are contemplating their whole life beyond school, to mid-life career changers, and seniors with time to devote to their hobbies.

As Figure B1 shows, people are working together to complete a wide range of different goals.

Reproduced by permission of 43Things.com

Figure B1

Dandelife.com

Dandelife is like the Timeline feature in Friends Reunited, but it tends to be used for more in-depth diary-like posts describing key life events. It integrates with Flickr and Youtube, so that you can combine video and photos from those sites with your stories. All the content is public, but comments are only allowed from registered members. Membership numbers are fairly low, but if you want to create a blog or write your life story, this is a platform worth considering.

Books & reading

Goodreads.com

Goodreads is a social network for book fans. Readers create virtual shelves of books they've read, or books they'd like to read, and can add their own reviews and comments on them. The site has over 2.5 million members who have added over 60 million books to their shelves, so you're sure to find somebody who can recommend something you'd like to read. More importantly, you can be alerted to reviews posted by your friends, which are likely to carry most weight with you.

Discussion groups centre on particular authors or genres, and you can also interact with authors who blog on the site.

Goodreads can update Twitter automatically with what you're reading and can tell your Facebook friends about your updates on Goodreads. There is integration with MySpace too, and a widget you can use in your Ning pages.

This is the most vibrant community connecting readers and writers, but similar sites include Library Thing (**www.librarything.com**, with 850,000 members) and Shelfari (**www.shelfari.com**, which is owned by Amazon).

Business

Linkedin.com

Many people have an informal network of friends and colleagues they can consult when they have questions about work and their professional development. LinkedIn brings these loose connections to the internet and enables you to consult your trusted network, and tap into the networks of your friends. Using LinkedIn, you can find new suppliers, clients, projects, employees and employers. LinkedIn also enables you to share your professional experience and expertise with others worldwide.

There are no games on LinkedIn; it's much more serious than Facebook or Friends Reunited. It is an ideal way to reconnect with former colleagues, and to collaborate with your social network on projects and professional development.

While there are some premium features on LinkedIn, you'll find that you can do most things you want to using a free account.

Disability

Disaboom.com

Disaboom is a website that connects people living with disability and anyone else touched by disability including friends and family, and healthcare professionals. The site claims to have 180 million members, which would make it one of the largest social networks covered in this book. The forums are friendly places to go for advice or a laugh, and members can share their experiences in groups, blog posts, live chats and photos.

Gardening

Growsonyou.com

Growsonyou is a friendly and supportive community of gardeners who share their tips and advice through blogs and question and answer forums. The site has 9,000 members, three-quarters of whom are over 40 years old. 65% of the members are female.

Photo sharing and commenting is a key part of the site. Members uploaded over 80,000 photos in the site's first two years. Growsonyou makes it easy to find pictures by colour or to find inspiring shots of small gardens, waterfalls or decking, among other design challenges.

The site is free to use. There is an optional garden supplies shop built-in.

Genealogy

Genesreunited.co.uk

Genesreunited is a sister site to Friends Reunited, dedicated to helping people to connect with their family members and create their family trees. The site has over 10.5 million members and enables you to search over 209 million names to see if your relations appear in other members' family trees. If they do, you can contact the member who owns that tree to find out more and view their family tree. The community shares tips on genealogy research, and there is pay-per-view and subscription access to scanned census records.

The site enables you to add your relatives to a world map and import or export data in the standard Gedcom format used by genealogy software.

Geni.com

This site has over 70 million profiles and enables families to collaborate to build their family tree online. Families can share photos and videos and add events to a timeline or calendar. Using Geni is a bit like having your own Ning network: there's no pre-built community for you because each family's discussion is private to them, so you'll need to invite others to join you if you're the first in your family to discover the site. You can do most things with a free account, but paid accounts start at $5 per month and provide access to advanced search and family tree statistics and also enable you to collaborate with others on your family tree. You can kickstart your tree with a Gedcom file if you've already been creating your tree using genealogy software or on another site that exports in that format.

Myheritage.com

This site has one foot in the past and one foot in the present. While the family tree is a key feature, the real focus of the site is on creating a mini website for your family to keep in touch. You can share photos, videos, recipes, polls, links, family news, and events on the calendar. The site includes facial recognition software which aims to make it easier to tag people in photographs, and to find photos of your family uploaded by other members. Your family website can be private or public. During the registration, the site railroads you into downloading a toolbar so you have all its tools always available in your browser, but this is optional. Just close your browser windows, open them up again and log in to the site and you can bypass the toolbar installation.

Knitting and crochet

Ravelry.com

Ravelry has 372,000 members who knit, spin, crochet or design patterns. On the site, you can share your projects with others, search for patterns and seek and share advice on the best tools and techniques. You can add other members as friends, and can join groups dedicated to chatting, swapping or local meets. The forums cover patterns, techniques, yarn, and needlework on the net.

Languages

Italki.com

Practising with a native speaker is the best way to keep your fluency up in a foreign language, and can also be a friendly way to improve your language skills if you're not yet fluent. Italki makes it easy for you to find study partners who are native speakers of the language you're learning, and who would benefit from your native language (probably English, if you're reading this).

Whatever you want to learn, you're bound to find a partner here: The site has over 450,000 members from 212 countries, who speak over 100 languages.

As well as finding language partners, you can join or start discussion forums (in English, or a foreign language) and can pose or answer questions about language study. There's a wiki for learning languages too, which is an encyclopaedia that anybody (including you) can edit. The ratings will help you to find the well researched and accurate entries. Don't forget the contributions mostly come from other students and might occasionally include errors – don't let their mistakes rub off on you!

Music

Last.fm

Last.fm is a site where music fans discuss their favourite artists and find others who share their tastes. There are groups where you can seek recommendations of new music to try, and Last.fm will itself analyse what you like and suggest new bands to you. If you listen to music on your computer, you can install software that keeps a record of what you play, which helps Last.fm create a personalised radio station you'll enjoy. If you want to blog about music, Last.fm enables you to create what it calls a journal and receive comments from other site members. When you visit other members' profiles, you can see how compatible your music tastes are, as Figure B2 shows:

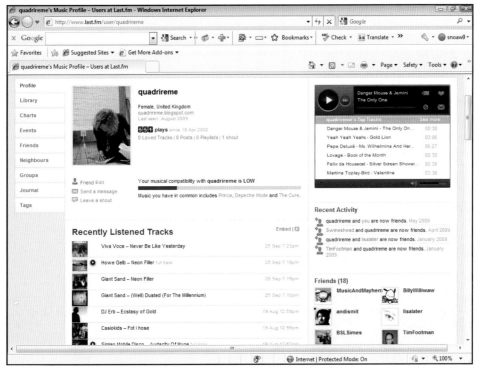

Reproduced by permission of Last.fm Ltd

Figure B2

Best of all, Last.fm will create a chart showing what you and your groups listen to most. Ready, pop pickers? Not 'arf!

MySpace.com

MySpace is the platform of choice for music fans and for musicians, both amateur and professional. Most big name acts have a presence there today, and new material is often released on the site first.

MySpace makes it easy to search for others in your age group, and to find new friends who are interested in friendship or dating. Bear in mind that many lie about their date of birth to protect their privacy, so the age displayed on a member's profile might be misleading. Either that, or it's the top hangout for young-looking septuagenarian dance music fans.

If you're a musician, comedian or film-maker, you can create a free MySpace profile that helps to promote your work. Anybody is welcome to join, blog on the site, and connect with friends.

MySpace members are guaranteed at least one friend. Tom Anderson, the site's co-founder, is automatically added to your friends list when you join up. Don't expect to hear from him much, though. He has over 260 million friends. That illustrates the difference between online friends and real friends perfectly.

News and views

Reddit.com and Digg.com

These are sites where people can share links to interesting stuff they've found on the internet, and vote on the links they like. They enable members to decide what's newsworthy, with the most popular links making it to the front pages. Each link has its own discussion thread, but the conversation can get rather fiery, particularly on political subjects on Digg. Discussions tend to focus on a single link, so there's not much repeated interaction with people unless you happen to be commenting on the same links. If you find someone you like though, you can see what else they've posted and this can be a good way to discover new websites, articles and videos you want to see.

Photography

Flickr.com

Flickr is dedicated to sharing and discussing photos. Now that digital cameras are relatively cheap (and even incorporated into phones and other devices), we are probably living at the most photographed time in history. Flickr makes it easy to share your memories, creative works and observations of daily life.

Members can tag areas of an image to comment on, perhaps drawing attention to a detail you might not have noticed, or comment on the image as a whole. While there is a wealth of public photos there, you can also use Flickr to create private groups for sharing and discussing photos of family occasions. There are groups dedicated to different types of photography, such as nature.

Flickr has a simple tool called Picnik for rotating, cropping, and resizing photos and for fixing colours and red-eye.

Normally copyright law means you're not allowed to republish someone else's pictures, but many members of Flickr make their images available for free under a creative commons licence. That means you can take those images from Flickr, with the creators' consent, and use them to decorate your profile or identify your group on other social networks.

Although most people access Flickr through its website, there are lots of different ways you can get photos in and out of Flickr. There is a Flickr application for Facebook, and a widget for Eons. You can customise your 43Things profile to display your photo stream in the sidebar. You can also add Flickr streams to your Ning social networks. For that reason, people often use Flickr as their main storage depot for photos, and let the images automatically flow from there into the other social networks they use.

Seniors

GrowingBolder.com

Growing Bolder is aimed at those who are 50+ and is a cross between a broadcaster and a social network. It has a team of professionals creating videos and audio programmes that tell inspiring stories related to wellness and positive living. Channels on the site enable quick access to professionally created and user generated content on the same subject. Those channels span a vast range of subjects, including a number of sports, health issues, entertainments, work issues, travel, technology and relationships. Social networking features include forums, blogs, groups, and photo galleries.

Travel

Couchsurfing.org

Couchsurfing is all about travelling the world, staying with hosts who donate the use of their couch (or spare room) for a night or two. The site has over a million members all over the world who are willing to offer up their couch for the night, or might like to sleep on yours. You're encouraged to spend time with your guest or host, and to use it as the chance to start a real-world friendship.

Safety is paramount, and the site has been designed with this in mind. The site is free to use, but members can offer a donation so they can be verified: Couchsurfing uses the payment details to validate that the member's name and address are true. Unlike most social networking sites, friends on Couchsurfing are people who know each other in the real world. Friends can vouch for each other, which enables other members to see how trustworthy somebody is. If somebody receives negative feedback, that also hurts the reputation of those who vouched for them, so it carries some weight. 99.6% of Couchsurfing experiences have been reported as positive on the site.

You don't have to host anyone you don't want to, and you can take the opportunity to just chat about travel in the discussion forums, or meet passing travellers for a coffee.

Couchsurfing has over one million members from 62,000 cities who speak 1,270 languages. If you've always wanted to go to Antarctica, and don't mind kipping on a sofa, then this could be your chance. Wrap up warm!

43Places.com

Sister site to 43Things (see biography section of this appendix), 43Places is a network for sharing your travel aspirations and experiences. The way the site works is similar to 43Things, and indeed you can share your login so you don't have to re-register. You can compile a list of places you want to visit and places you have already visited, and can share journal entries on both. The site is also a good place to go for suggestions on what you should see in a particular city.

As with 43Things, 43Places aims to inspire, giving you the ideas and encouragement to experience new countries, cultures and communities.

Travbuddy.com

Travbuddy enables travellers to share their travel stories, recommendations for places to see and photos from all over the world. The content is organised by location, with over 20,000 places recognised, making it the ideal place to go if you know you're travelling somewhere and want guidance on what to see. For photographers and travellers alike, the content is inspirational.

Travbuddy has over 1.5 million registered users, who have written 111,000 travel blogs and 32,000 travel reviews and have uploaded over 2 million photos of places all over the world. Membership is free.

Video sharing

Youtube.com

Youtube has brought about a revolution in how we consume television: many people are as likely to watch a few short films on Youtube a day as they are to sit down and watch a conventional TV broadcast. Those short films might be funny candids of everyday life, scripted mini-plays, business presentations or music performances.

Youtube video crazes often sweep the internet, such as Rickrolling (where people try to trick others into watching a Rick Astley video at Youtube) and the literal pop videos (where people caption pop videos and re-record the lyrics to match what is actually happening on screen, with often hilarious results).

Now that so many digital cameras and phones record video (check your manual, you might find yours does!), Youtube has been phenomenally successful. The site has 71 million different visitors each month and has been measured as the sixth most popular website in the world.

When you upload your video to Youtube, you can receive feedback from viewers and ratings out of five. As a viewer and film-maker, you can search by keyword for films you're interested in and participate in discussion groups.

Many other social networks rely on Youtube for their video functionality. If you want to add a video to Saga Zone or Meetup, for example, you need to upload it to Youtube first and then provide those sites with its address at Youtube. Only then can your friends discuss it and leave their comments on those sites.

Because Youtube is owned by Google, you can log in using your Googlemail/Gmail account, if you have one.

Virtual reality

SecondLife.com

Second Life is a virtual environment which you explore in 3D by moving your avatar around the screen, as shown in Figure B3.

Second Life is a trademark of Linden Research, Inc

Figure B3

The controls are like a computer game, with the freedom to walk, run and fly all over the world, but there's no goal to achieve. You can go there to do whatever you want: attend virtual concerts, explore the castles or hang out with friends in the parks.

Even though some social networks help you to shield your identity, most expect you to be yourself online. Second Life encourages you to create whatever virtual life you can imagine. It's a surreal fantasy land. You meet fox-headed gentlemen, daintily-dressed dames, dragons and funky dancers. Users can shape themselves in their own image, and adopt the personality, age and gender they would like to portray.

It's all built by users like you. In time, you could learn how to design your own clothes and buildings, and could even make money by creating objects and designs for other users. There is a whole economy in Second Life, with users exchanging Linden dollars (L$) for objects, clothes, building designs and services (such as DJ-ing or promotions work). You can use real money (including through Paypal) to buy in-game currency, and if you earn a decent amount, you can cash your L$ back into real money. Don't expect to get rich, though. There's a limit to how much people will pay for a bunch of pixels, however nicely arranged or animated they are.

You communicate in Second Life by typing and/or by speaking into a computer headset, similar to internet phone calls service Skype. Whichever you use, when you chat you can be heard by other avatars up to 20m away from you. If you shout (as frowned upon in Second Life as it is in the real world), you can be heard up to 100m away. If you want to communicate privately with someone, you use instant messages. It is possible to add characters to your friends lists, but is considered too forward to do that until you really are what could be considered friends. There are groups, which help you find other people who share your hobbies or interests.

Second Life is vast so you probably won't bump into the same people twice. Until you find your own regular haunt and make friends with the locals in-world, it's worth inviting offline friends to join you so you can explore together. You could sit side by side at the same computer, or log on separately (even from different countries) and arrange to meet up at the same place in the world.

When you get started, Second Life will introduce you to some places that offer informal training courses (mostly signs you read), and have a friendly welcome in the form of friendly tutors or Q&A sessions. I recommend the University of Oxbridge Course at Caledon as a good starting point.

To use Second Life, you'll need to register an account and install free software from the website at **www.secondlife.com**. For that reason, you'll probably need your own computer to use it. Membership is free and you can take advantage of all the features without buying any Linden dollars.

Some users of Second Life play out entire fictional life stories in the virtual world, including starting a business, buying some land, building their dream home and settling down with another player in a virtual marriage. The experience can be incredibly immersive. Just don't forget your first life!

Web surfing

Delicious.com

This site previously had the web address **del.icio.us**, but they have thankfully changed it to something we can all remember. Delicious enables you to share your web bookmarks online, and to find the websites that others are bookmarking. You describe sites using tags, short keywords of your own choice that summarise the content of a page. This site is best thought of as a people-powered search engine – it's good for finding new content, but the focus is very much on the bookmarks, rather than the community of people posting them.

StumbleUpon.com

If you enjoy surfing the web, StumbleUpon can give you tailored recommendations of new sites you'll enjoy. Members share their website bookmarks and reviews, and can give each webpage a 'thumbs up' or a 'thumbs down'. StumbleUpon works out a member's taste based on these ratings, and uses it to recommend websites that others with similar taste liked. It's a bit like Amazon's 'customers who bought this book, also bought this book' feature, only it's for website visits. There's a toolbar you can download, so you can give the thumbs up (or down) to any webpages you come across and stumble onto a new recommendation with a single click.

The site has over seven million members and has hundreds of different categories of website that you can express a preference for, when you register. These include home brewing, cats, lounge music, fishing, politics, weight loss, and rugby – there's something for everyone.

Integrating different social networks

Ping.fm

You probably want to go where your different groups of friends and favourite communities congregate, so that might mean using different networks at the same time. How can you manage the complexity of participating in multiple social networks? Ping.fm makes it easy to update different social networks with the same content, using a single interface.

At Ping.fm, you register your account details for major social networking sites. When you add text or photos to Ping, it then logs into your accounts and adds that content to your profiles for you.

While it doesn't support every site (Eons and Saga Zone are excluded, for example), it does include most mainstream social networks. Of those covered in this book, Ping.fm can post to Twitter, Facebook, LinkedIn, MySpace, Delicious, and Flickr.

Appendix: Glossary

application An extension to a social network, usually created by a different company from the one that built the network itself. Applications can add games, useful tools, or the ability to integrate information from other networks in one place. Social networks that support applications include Facebook and LinkedIn.

approve To authorise content written by somebody else before it is published. Social network members might have the right to approve comments written on their profile by their friends; and network organisers might choose to approve all blog posts. Some social networks also ask you to approve (accept) friend requests.

Back button A button on your browser which you click to go back to the previous page. Sometimes websites also include a Back button inside them too, to help you navigate a process that spans multiple web pages.

blog An easy way to publish content on the Internet, usually text and/or pictures, and automatically date-stamped. Can be used as a public diary, to share opinions, or to distribute creative works. Readers usually have the option to leave their comments. A blogger is someone who writes a blog.

bookmark A link to a web page stored in your browser so that you can quickly go back there.

breadcrumb trail A navigation tool on a website that shows how what you're looking at relates to other content on the site. It assumes the website is organised like Russian dolls, with sections inside sections. A trail might show

'Home >> Music >> Folk' if you were in the folk music section, for example. You could click Home to return to the front page, and Music to pick a different type of music.

broadband A fast connection to the Internet, which is permanently switched on so you can quickly view web pages, and download email, music, or video.

browser Short for web browser.

buzz A public greeting left on somebody's Friends Reunited profile.

chat A real-time exchange of messages between people on a social networking site. Chats can be public or private, and can be one-to-one or group. Everyone participating in a chat must be online at the same time. Chats are usually automatically deleted when they end.

click To 'click on a button' on a web page, you place your mouse cursor over that button image and then press the left button on your mouse.

clipboard A place for temporarily storing some content that you have copied or cut. The clipboard usually only stores the latest item, and if you copy or cut something else it will replace what was already on the clipboard.

comment Comments published in social networks are usually public.

Control key Marked CTRL, the Control key is used in combination with other keys to perform special functions. By holding down the Control key and tapping the V key, text can be pasted from the clipboard, for example.

copy To copy some content from one place and put it onto the clipboard, so that you can paste it in somewhere else. The content remains in its original location too. You can copy by highlighting the content you want and then using CTRL+C (the C stands for copy).

cursor The indicator of where you are on a web page. The mouse cursor moves with the mouse and transforms from an arrow to a hand when over a link. The text cursor is a blinking vertical line that shows where you are in a form or document.

cut To take some content from one place and put it onto the clipboard, so that you can paste it in somewhere else. The content you've cut is deleted from its original location if you have permission to do that. You can cut by highlighting the content you want and then using CTRL+X (the X is shaped like scissors).

digest Instead of receiving an email every time there is an update, you can often opt for a single daily or weekly email that combines all the updates in one message. This is known as a digest (because it is much easier to digest).

direct message A private message sent on Twitter. Can only be sent to your followers.

download To copy information from the Internet to your computer. Everything you access on the Internet is downloaded to your computer so you can view it.

email Short for electronic mail. An email is delivered to somebody's mailbox on the Internet for storage, until they can collect it using special PC software or by logging on to a website (if they are using webmail). Email is often used to update people about what is happening in their social networks and to prompt them to log in and respond.

email address An email address is used to route emails to the person you want to receive them. An email address always includes an @ sign and doesn't have any spaces in it. You can get a free email address from webmail providers such as Googlemail (**www.googlemail.com**). Your Internet Service Provider usually provides one or more email addresses with your Internet connection too.

flame An abusive, aggressive, or angry comment directed at another member of a social networking site. When flames are reciprocated and escalate, a flame war is said to have broken out.

follower Somebody who subscribes to your updates on Twitter. While you can block unwanted followers, you do not get to approve followers in the same way that you approve friend requests.

form Like a paper form, an onscreen form includes boxes for you to fill in your information. The form can include text boxes, radio buttons, tick boxes, and pull-down menus. At the bottom of the form there is usually a button to click to save your changes or submit your information.

forum A place online where people discuss subjects by posting messages and comments which are stored on the site. Because the messages are stored, the discussion can go on for weeks and involve many people who log on to the forum at different times.

friend Somebody you are directly connected to on a social network. Being friends on a social network usually means that you share more information with each other, so both parties must agree to the relationship. An online friend is not always somebody who is a friend in the real world.

friend request An invitation from one member of a social network to another to become friends. If accepted, both members can access more of each other's information.

group A subset of members of a social network who share a particular interest and use dedicated tools provided (such as group chat and forums) to communicate with each other.

highlight To select text or graphics so that you can cut or copy them. To highlight content, move the mouse to its start, click the left mouse button, and drag the mouse to the end of the content.

Home The browser's Home button takes you to your browser's start page. Inside a website, the homepage is used to refer to the main starting page of a website. If you get lost, clicking the Home link inside a website will take you back to the beginning.

Inbox Where messages and action items (such as outstanding event invitations and friend requests) in a social network are often stored. Also the word for where emails arrive when they are first delivered.

Instant Messaging (IM) A PC-based technology for sending text messages immediately to a friend's screen. Programs that enable IM include Windows Messenger and AOL Instant Messenger.

Internet A network that connects computers together so that they can exchange information, including emails and web pages.

Internet Explorer A leading web browser created by Microsoft.

Internet Service Provider (ISP) A company that rents you a connection to the Internet. Often the same company as your telephone line provider.

JPEG A compressed format for pictures, commonly used for photographs.

keywords Words describing something you're looking for in a search engine, or words others might use to do the same.

link A path between two web pages, either on the same site or on different sites. When you click a link, your web browser takes you to the page it is connected to. Links can be text (such as 'Video' to go to the video section) or can be images (such as a picture of a television). On a well-designed website it should be obvious what is a link, but you can be sure you are on a link if your mouse cursor turns into a hand. Text links are often in blue text and underlined. They often change colour after you've visited them.

log in/log out When you arrive at a social network, you need to tell it who you are so it can provide you with your content. That is known as logging in. To stop others from using your account on your PC while you're away, you should log out when you've finished.

LOL Short for "laughing out loud", used in chats and forums.

mailing list A way for members of a group to have a discussion by email. They send a single message to the mailing list, and the list software forwards a copy of it to everybody on the list. Mailing lists are also used by organisers in social networks to broadcast messages to their members.

message If a social network's 'Message' function is used, the communication is usually private between the sender and recipient.

message board Another term for a forum.

moderation The practice of policing content on a social network to make sure that it doesn't breach the community's standards. Should also be exercised with regard to eating biscuits.

MP3 A file format that enables music to be compressed for distribution over the Internet.

navbar Short for navigation bar, the navbar is the main control panel for moving around the site. It includes text or image links to the main sections. By convention, navbars tend to run across the top of a website, or down the left-hand side. They can appear anywhere, though.

News Flash Friends Reunited's term for a status update.

NSFW "Not safe for [viewing at] work." A warning of potentially offensive content.

OMG Short for "Oh my God!", used in chats and forums.

online On the Internet. If a person is shown as online in a social network, it means they are using that website now too. If some content is described as being online, it means you can download it over the Internet.

organiser The manager of a social network or group, usually with the power to edit or delete content, and to ban and manage members.

password Like a key protects a building, a password protects your account and stops others from gaining access without your permission. Since only you should know your password, providing it proves that you are who you claim to be and are authorised to access the information requested. Your passwords should be hard for others to guess and easy for you to remember.

paste To move some content from the clipboard to where your cursor is. The content remains on the clipboard too, so you can paste it into multiple different places. To paste, use CTRL+V (located next to the X and C used to cut and copy).

PayPal A company that enables people to send money to each other, or to companies, over the Internet. Owned by eBay and often used for online auction payments.

PC Short for personal computer.

PDF A format for sending documents over the Internet that preserves their layout so they print well. Usually used to reproduce print documents where the layout is significant. To read PDFs you need to install the free Acrobat Reader program from **www.adobe.com**.

PIN Personal Identification Number. Performs the same function as a password.

plug-in An extension to a web browser that enables it to handle new types of content or to perform new functions, such as browsing and uploading photos.

poll A simple multiple choice survey, often used to solicit feedback from the community on events ideas or to kick-start a discussion.

pop-up menu A new menu that appears when you hover over a particular part of the screen.

post A single piece of content added to a social networking site, such as a blog entry or a contribution on a forum. Adding content to social networks is sometimes called posting.

privacy settings Used to restrict who can view your content in a social network.

profile Your own description of yourself, which can be read by other members of your social network. Often includes a summary of your latest activity on that network too.

program A set of instructions for the computer that enable it to achieve a set of related tasks. You might have a program for word processing, writing and reading email, or playing Sudoku.

pull-down menu A menu that unrolls and presents its options to you when you click on it. Pull-down menus keep the screen tidy by hiding options until you need them.

radio button Radio buttons are round and are used to select one from a number of options. If you click one radio button in a group, it will deselect the previous radio button you had selected (if any). Might be used on a form that asks if you are male or female, for example.

Refresh button Button on the web browser. When it is clicked, the browser downloads the current web page again, including any updates to it since the last time it was downloaded.

ROFL or ROTFL Short for "rolling on the floor laughing", used in chats and forums.

save To preserve some information permanently. If you make changes to your social network profile, for example, they might be discarded when you leave the web page if you do not click the Save button first.

scroll To move a document that won't all fit on screen at once so that you can see a different part of it. Usually used to scroll a long web page that spills off the bottom of the screen. Contents can be scrolled using the scrollwheel between the buttons on the mouse, or by clicking and dragging the scrollbars down the right and/or along the bottom of a window.

search engine A tool for finding what you need inside a website, or on the Internet as a whole. You type in keywords that summarise what you want and then click the button to request the search results. Sometimes you can use advanced options to narrow your search to particular types of content or date ranges.

site Short for website.

smiley Sometimes known as an emoticon. A textual representation of an emotion, such as :-). Although known as smileys, they can also be sad :-(.

social network A website that provides tools to help people to communicate with groups of family and friends, and with groups of people they don't yet know who share their interests.

spam Junk email or another unsolicited direct advertising communication. Not the same as advertising on the site which is legitimately sold by the site's owners and used to keep the site free for everyone. Advertising subsidises content. Spam just leaches off the communications infrastructure.

spammer Somebody who sends spam.

status update A short message you add to your profile to say what you're doing, thinking or feeling, such as "Sean is writing a glossary". Sometimes others can comment on your status updates. Some networks archive them permanently on the profile, while others only display the latest update. Pioneered by Facebook, status updates now feature in most social networks.

submit To send the information in your form to the website. When you have finished filling in a form, you must sometimes click the Submit button to send that data.

tab The term 'tab' is taken from a filing cabinet metaphor. If you are using multiple websites in the browser, click a web page's tab to bring it to the front. Inside a website, tabs are sometimes used to navigate between different sections of the site. Clicking them sometimes brings up a new navbar for moving around that section of the site.

tag This has two different meanings: a short description of some content used to make it easier to find; or a special code used to describe how some content should be presented (such as in bold text).

tagging Adding short descriptions to online content so it can be found more easily and can be associated with related content. Social networks often encourage you to tag photos with the names of people in them, so that these people can quickly find them.

text box Has two different meanings: generally, a space on a web page where you can enter text content such as your name; specifically on Ning, also a tool used to add widgets to a network.

thread A set of linked messages that belong to the same discussion, which is either private or public. If you reply to a post or message, your reply is added to its thread.

thumbnail A small preview version of a photograph so you can see if it's what you want before you download the full-size version. Usually at least twice the size of a thumbnail (unless you have hands like a shovel).

tick box Used on a form to indicate multiple items. On a menu with tick boxes, you could choose to tick multiple items. Sometimes called a check box, the square tick boxes are not to be confused with the round radio buttons, which only enable one option to be chosen.

troll Someone who goes into a forum or chat and posts messages designed to start a fight. This is known as trolling.

tweet A public message published on Twitter. Tweets have a maximum length of 140 characters.

upload To copy information from your computer to the Internet. You might upload photos from your computer to your social network profile, for example.

URL Short for Uniform Resource Locator, this is the same as a web address.

username How you identify yourself to a social network. Your username must be unique so that your content doesn't get mixed up with someone else's.

wall A space on somebody's profile where anyone who can view it is allowed to leave a public comment.

Web Short for World Wide Web, the part of the Internet that most people use. For the average Internet user, the Web and the Internet are pretty much the same thing.

web address Also known as a URL, this is the unique location on the Internet of a particular web page. It appears in the address bar, and is what you bookmark if you add a web page to your Favorites. To visit a different web page, you can type or paste its web address into the address bar.

web browser The program used to navigate the Internet. Web browsers are usually free to download and include Internet Explorer. Often called just a 'browser'.

webcam A camera that is permanently connected to the computer, usually to enable video messages to be sent. Can also be used to take still photographs for use in social networking sites.

webmail A website that enables you to read and write, send and receive emails. You don't need to install any software and can access webmail anywhere you can access the Internet. Examples include Googlemail (**www.googlemail.com**).

web page A page downloaded from the Internet, which can include text, pictures, videos, music, forms, animations, and interactive features (such as games). A web page might not fit on screen at once, so it might need to be scrolled to see all of it.

website A group of linked web pages that are operated by the same person and are about the same thing. Most organisations have a single website that hosts all their public-facing activities on the Internet. Anybody is allowed to create a website.

widget A small piece of website functionality that you can incorporate (or 'embed') into a web page or social network by copying and pasting a short snippet of code. Widgets might include games, photos, or headlines from other websites.

window A window is an onscreen box that a single program runs in. A browser window provides you with a view of a single website.

Windows Microsoft Windows (aka Windows) is what you see when you switch on most PCs: it provides the controls you need to manage your files and programs.

WTH Short for "what the hell!", used in chats and forums.

WWW An abbreviation for World Wide Web.

zoom To enlarge a web page or photo so that it's easier to read or view.

Index